The Opportunity Maker

Strategies for Inspiring Your Legal Career

Through Creative Networking and Business Development

By

Ari L. Kaplan

Mat #40748801

© 2008 Thomson/West
    610 Opperman Drive
    St. Paul, MN 55123
    1–800–313–9378

Printed in the United States of America

ISBN: 978–0–314–19442–8

TEXT IS PRINTED ON 10% POST CONSUMER RECYCLED PAPER

For Lauren

For so many reasons . . .

ACKNOWLEDGMENTS

When Erin Shanahan (now with the Source Books division of Sphinx Publishing) e-mailed me in the summer of 2006 asking if I was interested in writing this book, I rejected the offer outright. I did not have the time, I did not know how to write a book (a point with which you may agree after reading the first few pages), and I did not have anything worthy to share. Erin persisted and eventually I gave in. Although she is no longer with my publisher, I owe her a debt of gratitude for promoting this project. I also owe a similar debt to Rebecca Luczycki of the National Jurist for sharing my article on rainmaking with Erin and to Ira Pilchen of the ABA Student Lawyer magazine for asking me to write about the subject.

To all of those I interviewed, it is your insight, experience and guidance from which the readers will benefit. It was a privilege learning from you and I am grateful for your time and assistance.

A special note of appreciation for their confidence in me to Sharon Abrahams, Lisa Horowitz, JeanMarie Campbell, Olivia Freeman, Diane Barrasso, Jane Rhee, Nakia Humphrey, Susan Schoenfeld, Beverly Hedrick, Molly Peckman, Rebecca Matthews, Andrea Jacobson, Bari Chase, Richard Demb, Gabe Galanda, Kate Holmes, Mike Kinnaman, Maria Rutkin, Naila Maroon, David Snow, Christy Burke, Randy Lee, Kendall Coffey, Debbie Caldwell, Jeanette Slepian, Prashant Dubey, Sean Carter, Kevin Reifler, Carla Main, Paul Cappuccio, Steve Weiser, and my two excellent assistants from NYU, Angela Zhu and Josephine Tung.

Also, to Mark Moran, Terry Moran and the team at findingDulcinea for encouraging my completion of this book; to Stacey Gray for sharing her remarkable network; and, to my mentor, Lisa Linsky, for having faith in me even when I lacked it in myself. To Alex Hanan, David Liss, Josh Losardo, Zachary Prell, Ruddy Reyes, Josh Rothman, Danny Rootenberg, John Weinshank, and Danny Weiss—for your friendship.

Thanking Lauren, my wife, and our children, Emory and Hannah, for their patience every time an interview ran long and they were waiting in the car or had to go somewhere without me because I had a section of this book to finish is insufficient. They inspire me every day. Professor Jeanne Paratore of Boston University once told me that coming home to her children was like opening up a present every single day. I could not agree more. They are a great gift and I write to create a legacy for them.

To my sister, Bonni, my uncle, Jeff, Esther, Richie, Harry, Robyn, Arnie, Terry, Bobby, David, Bubby, and, of course, Shari. I am lucky to have you in my life. To my mother, Felice, and my grandmother, Gert, thank you for raising me, protecting me, motivating me and loving me; my dad, Mike, for changing the course of my future by altering the course of his; and, finally, Emanda. It is in my soul that I miss you most, but am always comforted by your presence. I write to reach you and hope that you receive the messages I send through my words.

And, because I can never say it too many times ... for Lauren, for always.

About the Author

As the principal of Ari Kaplan Advisors, Mr. Kaplan counsels professionals internationally on the art of getting published and dynamic networking. He teaches techniques for leveraging writing and embracing other activities as the foundation for business development. His in-house training programs, personal coaching and corporate writing projects communicate his methods.

The author subscribes to his training philosophy. He has published over 150 articles, served as a legal commentator for CNET Radio, hosted a public access cable television show in Manhattan, taught Internet law at Baruch College, and founded the Ari Kaplan Advisors charitable book collection through the Intergenerational Literacy Project in Chelsea, Massachusetts.

Mr. Kaplan is a member of the Board of Editors for ALM Media's Marketing the Law Firm and Legal Tech. He has been interviewed on CNN and was named a "Law Star" by LawCrossing. He is also the recipient of a 2007 Apex Award recognizing his marketing article for Small Firm Business magazine, "How To Stand Out From a Crowd."

Mr. Kaplan practiced law in New York City for nearly nine years and is admitted to the bar in New York, New Jersey and Washington, D.C. He earned his J.D. from George Washington University Law School and his B.A., magna cum laude, from Boston University.

Learn more about the author at AriKaplanAdvisors.com and the principles in this book at TheOpportunityMaker.com.

The Opportunity Maker
Table of Contents

Chapter 5

Chapter 6

Chapter 7

Chapter 8

Chapter 9

Chapter 10

Chapter 11

Chapter 12

Chapter 13

Chapter 14

Chapter 15

Chapter 16

Chapter 17

Introduction
THE $100/MONTH BUSINESS DEVELOPMENT PROMISE

I once read in a magazine when I was 25 that if you put $100 per month into an average stock mutual fund, you will have $1 million at 65. I never quite understood the math, but that is after all why I went to law school. Still, I have been paying into that fund for about ten years now and in about three decades I will let you know the result. The same investment principle applies to your future, though if the time period were as long, you would be retired before seeing your name listed on any firm's letterhead.

Most of those already on the letterhead realized early on that the art of business development is actually a science. I have often wondered why some lawyers had clients and others simply yearned helplessly for them. I learned that it was partly talent, but not mythical ability. It was partly luck, but not the type characterized by lottery winners. And, it was partly personality. Okay, that last one might be a stretch for some, but there is a certain level of enthusiasm that attracts clients to one lawyer over another.

I never quite identified the exact formula because it was never the same. The common trait amongst all of the people I thought of as rainmakers was this: they started early and they were committed to success, not unlike my $100 monthly contribution.

Instead of money, I suggest that you pay into the fund of your future by trying the techniques proposed in this book on a monthly basis, and perhaps more frequently. They include uncommon ways of finding success in common strategies. Get yourself a business card, say some experts. Take a course in marketing, say others. Why didn't I think of that?

Start a blog, create an association, read; the list goes on and on.

If you think self-promotion is for partners, you are right. If you think you can wait until you become a partner (or even a licensed attorney for that matter) to start planting seeds, you have never been more wrong.

Self-promotion is part of the art of lawyering. There is no 3-credit class on the subject, but it is as critical to legal practice as torts and contracts. The best lawyers are great at what they do and at conveying that greatness to others.

I spoke with many of the great ones and with an elite group of business development visionaries, not for their secrets, but for their practical advice on the steps that you can take right now to control your destiny. I also spoke with students and new lawyers who successfully subscribe to my theory. Look at it this way: If the book doesn't help, at least you got some Warren Buffet-esque investing advice right up there in the first paragraph.

The Relationship Between Self-Promotion and Rainmaking

People often wonder what the direct correlation is between organically promoting yourself and client generation. Those who do the wondering tend to fail before they start. This book is not about how to neatly get from point A to point B. It is about how to navigate the roller coaster ride from point A to point B by choosing your own path to that destination. It will help you identify what works for your style and how to effectively implement certain creative strategies to generate opportunities. Understanding the techniques that others have used and continue to apply in their quest will help you set milestones on the road ahead.

The relationship between self-promotion and rainmaking is simple: those who can genuinely engage with others tend to be more satisfied, more excited about their work and more fulfilled in how they live. Those qualities attract opportunities, which are often converted into professional success. We want to believe that it is more complicated than that to explain why so few people master the art. The truth is: They master the art because they concern themselves with the journey rather than the destination.

On your journey, always keep your umbrella handy as a reminder of the rain that is to come. Meet people to learn about them, not so that they will become a client. Be charitable because it is worthwhile, not because it will impress prospects. Get creative because it will enhance your work and inspire your day, not to attract business.

My grandmother used to always tell me, "don't worry, success will come." I share that advice with you. If you don't believe me, I had the good fortune to learn from over 100 people featured in this book who concur. They know what works and are happy to convey it to you.

Chapter 1
THE MOST IMPORTANT LESSON LAW SCHOOL NEVER TEACHES

I remember sitting in Contracts II my second semester in law school wondering, "What the heck am I going to use this knowledge for?" Granted, the brightest guy in my class was going to practice con law. The rest of us were focusing on something more common like business planning or personal injury. Essentially, the bread and butter stuff that makes good fodder for the "how many lawyers does it take to…" jokes.

During the daydreams, my second question was always, "How am I ever going to get a client to pay me for this?" (My third question was, of course, "Why did I go to law school?" but I normally shook that one off because it popped into my head during every class, exam and annoying conversation with the study group outline gatekeepers.) If my school had a seminar, class or even a required conversation with a professor on answering the issue that plagued me, the others might have gone away.

That's where this book comes in.

While a couple of visionary law schools have engaged experts to teach non-credited seminars on planting seeds, the idea is a complete non-starter for the vast majority. "Many law schools are thirsty to have programs that distinguish them," says Nancy Robert Linder, a consultant from La Grange, IL who teaches business development at Chicago-Kent and Valparaiso.

I didn't love law school, but it did teach me the law, how to convey that law to clients, judges and peers, and even a little something about negotiation and public speaking. (Bet you wish I learned a little bit more about writing.)

The one thing it did not teach me (and this is actually a big one) is how to promote myself to prospects and the community at large. Frankly, law school, my pedagogical nemesis, that was an important point to forget.

Since all barrister-producing institutions follow the same teaching patterns, there are over a million lawyers in the United States alone without a clue how to make it drizzle, let alone rain. Of course, knowing how to make it rain is only important if you want to control your own destiny and pay back your loans before your kids go to law school.

There is a common misconception that business development is about selling, but it is much more about knowing. Knowing yourself, knowing your capabilities and knowing where they are best suited.

1.1 The Art of Rainmaking

A partner I worked with once told me that you'll never worry about being promoted if you have your own clients. But alas, law students and lawyers worry. It is the essence of the profession. We worry about passing classes, then the bar. We worry about getting a job, then looking for a new one. And, at some point, we worry about getting a client, then another.

We study to pass exams and we prepare for job interviews. We do not, however, do much, if anything at all, for that third set of worries which is just as critical as the first two.

Some people are different. 32-year-old partner Gabe Galanda of Seattle's Williams Kastner has over a million dollars' worth of business from clients that include publicly traded companies, banks, apparel retailers, insurance firms and twelve tribal governments. A descendant of the Nomlaki and Concow Tribes and enrolled member of the Round Valley Indian Tribes in the Pacific Northwest, he has solidified himself as an authority on Indian Law, published scores of articles and is a leader in local, regional and national bar associations. The University of Arizona Rogers College of Law alumnus has spent the eight years since his graduation on the critically important journey toward securing his future (and he's just getting started).

Galanda is not successful by accident. He was interested in Indian Law in law school. Upon graduation, he fueled his interest by associating with others in the field, writing about related topics, and seeking out speaking opportunities. He did not set out to be a rainmaker; he set out to enjoy the practice by doing what he wanted instead of what someone determined that he should do. That is the art of rainmaking.

Veteran rainmaker, Angelo Paparelli, founder of the bi-coastal immigration firm of Paparelli & Partners LLP echoes that sentiment. "Start by doing that which you already enjoy," he suggests. "The practice of law that involves what you love doing is the best practice."

1.1.1 WHAT IS RAINMAKING?

The term "rainmaking" is probably defined differently in the industry, but it carries with it one central theme: independence. In its most basic form, rainmaking is client development. It is the skill for repeatedly generating business with relative ease and confidence.

Here is an easy way to understand this principle: Lawyers who work on matters generated by other lawyers typically have a job as long as their peers value that work. But, lawyers who generate their own work have a job as long as they want and, therefore, control their own future.

That is rainmaking.

The journey toward becoming a rainmaker requires a creative vision. It does not require unconventional methods, but it does crave consistency and evolution for success.

It also requires a certain self-transformation. Law students are trained to be conservative and risk averse. Creative self-promotion is all about calculated risk. The two may seem to be in conflict, but they are very much in sync for business development. One must transform one's thinking from the law to the business of law, and from demonstrating knowledge to conveying knowledge.

That transformation will only come with a yearning for empowerment. There are frightening statistics about lawyers and the rate of depression. Many of those cases are probably due to the sense of helplessness lawyers feel at a certain point in their careers, i.e., they cannot go backward or move forward. Those seeking empowerment know that forward momentum is the only option, and that process begins in law school.

Budding barristers can begin building momentum and empowerment in daily rituals that enhance control of the present and the future. Being elected to the partnership is a worthy accomplishment based on billable hours, but without contributing to the growth of the firm by acquiring new business, you remain remotely expendable and, therefore, insecure. True control comes with contribution, which in law-firm-speak means business generation.

Business generation sounds like a daunting task, but it is only a matter of unleashing talent. The idea of rainmaking is a secret in many firms. A handful of lawyers often bring in the clients. The remaining attorneys are kept too busy to focus on anything but the work. They have the talent, the connections and the drive to do so, but have not yet unleashed their ability.

By learning who you are and what you offer most, you can sharpen your business development talent now, instead of the day after you "make" partner at a firm or decide it is time for you to open your own shop. The steps are not that complicated, but they do require a plan. They also require a sense of altruism.

Many professionals think that doing favors for others is a good way to get business, but actually doing favors for others is a good way to live. The same is true for law students, who in many ways have more to give and less to sacrifice.

The return will come in ways you do not expect, so strategizing before doing is pointless. For example, if you find a new business idea interesting, call the founder and suggest that you meet for an interview and then write an article. Maybe he or she will someday become a client, maybe not. One thing is for sure, he or she will now be part of your network, which as you will see, is incredibly valuable.

What rainmaking is not is being everything to everyone. It is not meeting people for the sake of having their name in your phonebook. It is not keeping in touch with every member of your first year section or spamming the entire ABA Young Lawyers Division. There is a great scene from the movie "Singles" where one of the characters collects the phone numbers of women that he has met at a nightclub in his Casio digital watch. He boasts about his successful collection of 20 numbers to his friend, who (if I may paraphrase) replies, "You now have 20 numbers of 20 women that you are never going to call."

Don't construct a network—build relationships. Don't just join someone's LinkedIn profile; meet in person whenever you can. Find reasons to interact with people. Seek out opportunities to do someone a favor.

Remind people of your periodic accomplishments. This means you need to have such accomplishments, but we'll get into that later. In addition, contact people for informational interviews, guidance on a law review article or assistance with a pro bono case. These types of inquiries are non-invasive, completely work-related and foster continued dialogue. They are ideal for making connections.

Connecting with others and rainmaking in general are critical both for your development and success. Once lawyers are well into their careers, they obsess over rainmaking like it is a trick they can learn quickly. Most are frustrated because it is more like long-term investing than solving the Rubik's Cube. It needs to be honed and crafted over the course of a lifetime, rather than called on when necessary.

In fact, for the best rainmakers, the art of business development is more about relationship cultivation. It is a lifestyle, not a burden. It is an opportunity to make friends and to live a much more exciting existence within the law.

1.1.2 WHERE TO START

Every lawyer, non-lawyer and person that knows a lawyer or non-lawyer will tell you that the first rule for becoming a rainmaker is to study, learn the law and master the techniques of lawyering. "The number one priority for law students is to become the best lawyers they can. You cannot gain the respect of your colleagues if your legal skills are not up to par," says Felice Wagner of Washington, D.C.-based Sugarcrest Development Group, a client development training and consultancy firm for lawyers. The key factor in all business development is that an individual has the talent to properly assist a client. So invest the time it takes to do well your first year.

That said, it used to be that 1Ls were limited to subscribing to legal publications and learning to "talk the talk." Today, however, activities like blogging offer a powerful way for students and practitioners alike to market without lifting a finger (well at least not from their keyboards).

Steve Rubel, Senior Vice President at New York City-based Edelman, a global public relations firm, started blogging in April of 2004. Encouraged by the 25-50 hits he was receiving per day, the then-unknown Rubel continued sharing his ideas with the tiny crowd on how social media was transforming marketing and public relations. Then he got creative.

Rubel contacted the Poynter Institute, a St. Petersburg, Florida-based journalism school and think tank, in June of 2004 and proposed a story on the "All Blog Media Diet," an experiment that would have him refrain from any news sources other than blogs for one week. (In early 2004, this was a novelty.) "It was not designed to be frivolous; it made a point," notes Rubel. Apparently it worked, because as of November, 2007, his blog, Micropersuasion.com, was getting 100,000 page views per month and had 25,000 subscribers. "It is like I am going into Madison Square Garden and I am writing," he says and compares blogging at his level to the equivalent of national TV on the Internet.

His advice for students and lawyers alike is to find a niche, be dedicated and stay active. Even 1Ls can do that—just take a look at the growing number of law student blogs listed on Technorati.

Famed blawging evangelist, Kevin O'Keefe agrees with Rubel. "You have to engage in the online discussion to exist," says the founder of LexBlog. The truth is that more people are going to be interacting online than anywhere else. Some lawyers are even using MySpace and YouTube to market their skills (more on that later). Contrary to what your CivPro professor told you, O'Keefe, a former trial attorney, recommends that students and junior associates "stop thinking like a lawyer and start thinking more like a person."

While ingrained, the "thinking like a lawyer" paradigm is exactly what transforms otherwise capable rainmakers into law firm billing machines with no career control whatsoever. If you have the wrong map of your future, looking harder is of no use. I always seem to read discouraging statistics about lawyers having the highest rate of depression, but when you think about it, spending your career searching for something you will never find because you have no idea where to look is a pretty grim task that would make Sisyphus long for the boulder.

The key is to create a plan and pursue it relentlessly with great passion and enthusiasm. Ultimately, this will bear fruit from a business and professional perspective, but will likely have a wide-ranging impact on your personal development as well.

Rubel suggests taking chances early by meeting new people through teaching, attending events targeted at those more experienced and studying other industries to learn what is happening outside of the law. He also notes that without sacrificing a minute of training, students and early associates can grow their creative minds. The billable hour notwithstanding, everyone has a few minutes per day to appreciate a piece of music, a great poem or an inspiring profile. It simply needs to be incorporated more actively into a daily routine.

STUDENTS TAKE NOTE: Students should behave. Wagner says that students should monitor their conduct in law school because "stupid behavior in law school can come back to haunt you. Ten years down the road, you won't get business because people think you are an idiot." If you're a perennial goof, this book isn't going to help. If, however, you're overwhelmed by the possibilities, read on and take it slow.

1.1.3 WHAT ARE THE MECHANICS?

1.1.3.1 BECOME A GREAT LAWYER

Law students and junior associates work hard to complete assigned tasks under their deadlines and at the highest level of quality. Those with visions of becoming rainmakers do their work, seek out additional projects and study them in earnest. "If you do a really good job and partners use you as the go-to person, inevitably you are going to catch a break," says Tonya Grindon, a partner with Baker, Donelson, Bearman, Caldwell & Berkowitz, PC in Nashville, TN.

The best rainmakers-to-be read case briefs about developments in their area of the law, available in most law school and firm libraries, as well as online. Visit sites like Findlaw.com to gauge the possibilities. Findlaw may also give you ideas for trade magazines and other periodicals in which you might be interested. So, if you are interested in sports law, pick up a copy of The Sporting News as well as a treatise on the subject.

In addition to studying substantive material, "tag along" on important hearings, client meetings, and work-related events. Just watching a senior attorney argue before a judge is experience that can shape your skill set. These opportunities are often a phone call or a mouse click away. Find out in advance when these events are set to occur and contact the responsible attorney. Few will decline the opportunity to have an audience.

Summer associates can really distinguish themselves with this level of enthusiasm, and newly minted legal eagles might be able to take this one step further by assisting with a pro bono assignment that might provide a rare oral argument or client counseling session.

1.1.3.2 MAKE PRESENTATIONS

Presentation opportunities knock softly when you are in school or when you first start practicing, so listen closely. If a clinic professor, internship supervisor or a partner asks you to prepare PowerPoint slides for a presentation, client meeting or a continuing legal education course, make the best slides you possibly can. Similarly, if as the most junior member of a bar association committee, you are asked to speak about an issue you are researching, make it good. The number of people you address is unimportant.

"I have spoken to groups ranging in size from twelve people at the Department of Defense for an Indian law celebration to 700 franchise lawyers at a conference because I always assume that there is a potential client or a referral source in the audience—it is six degrees of separation kind of stuff," Galanda says.

At the beginning of your career, just get visible. That visibility will create dividends later when you are a more established practitioner.

Enterprising individuals will contact partners that make presentations and ask to assist them on a future project only to learn that those partners are all too happy to utilize the offer of free assistance. This is an especially valuable technique for law students (particularly those in their third year) who have the time to give. Those who know the specific area in which they are interested should contact local community associations or business groups and offer to speak at the next meeting. Lawyers in your network or those serving as mentors are a good source of information on these opportunities.

1.1.3.3 JUST GET INVOLVED IN SOMETHING

Pending and recent graduates should get involved in activities and associations because "it forces you to meet people and practice relationship-building tools," says Linder. Galanda revitalized Seattle's Northwest Indian Bar Association. What had been a collection of twenty-one names on a largely dormant e-mail list has become a thriving group of hundreds of lawyers with a common interest across the country. "I studied Indian law and tapped into a tribal network nationally," recalls Galanda. "I created opportunities for myself to be viewed by the tribal public, members of which constituted prospective and now current clients."

You do not need to start your own bar association, but you should join something, preferably local because membership in your city bar may initially provide access to contacts that have a greater impact on your business development or initial job search than a state bar membership. If you are more interested in spending time with non-lawyers in a particular field, find a copy of the Encyclopedia of Associations at your local or firm library and identify a group with which you would like to become affiliated.

According to Wagner, whether you engage in a bar association, chamber of commerce or even community-focused activities, how you perform your functions in the association will be measured and watched closely. "People will use that as a proxy as to how you will do as their lawyer," she says. "Folks that are most successful at using an association membership for getting business are involved and committed," she adds.

1.1.3.4 BUILD RELATIONSHIPS

Many people believe that making as many contacts as possible is a valuable form of self-promotion, but that is not enough. Linder recommends that lawyers help, learn from and listen to prospective clients. "The practice of law is a relationship business," she says. Relationships start with an initial meeting, but are nurtured by follow-up and commitment.

Law students can develop this technique by creating a contact list of friends and colleagues. Let these people know when you publish, speak and achieve professional milestones. Periodically send them articles that may be of interest to them, whether written by you or not. Some law students set goals to have lunch with someone new once per month and then increase the frequency of that practice as they become more established.

One important point for new lawyers is that "your clients in a firm are the other lawyers inside of a firm," says Wagner. "You want to be the go-to associate because down the road that will make you the go-to partner," she adds. The same is true for a law student clerking in the summer and during the school year.

Write your personal bio for the firm's website and update it as the need arises. Consider maintaining a separate website that contains a resume and an archive of your work, but ensure its professionalism. If your personal Web page would negatively reflect on your candidacy at a job interview, take it down.

In addition, volunteer to assist with your organization's marketing efforts by either contacting your firm's marketing director or reaching out to a knowledgeable partner.

1.1.3.5 PERFECT YOUR PITCH

One of the best techniques that young lawyers can master is creating a brief summary pitch about who they are and what they do. "You want to be remembered and establish a connection such that when there is a need, you are the first person someone thinks of," Galanda remarks. Wagner echoes this point noting, "People are evaluating you every step of the way."

Practice your pitch in front of the mirror or by setting up a video camera at home and recording your self-introduction. Galanda recommends that you learn how to navigate a cocktail party. "Bring your business card and figure out how you are going to introduce yourself in 20 seconds," he says.

When David Schnurman graduated from New York Law School in May of 2006 and founded TrueNYC, he embraced this concept. His popular public access cable television program in Manhattan, features interviews with prominent and emerging entrepreneurs.

To expand on his interviewing concept, Schnurman is now empowering self-marketing law students by creating video resumes. New York Law School began piloting this program for its students in September of 2006.

1.2 WHO ARE THE BEST RAINMAKERS
OR ON TRACK TO BE THE BEST?

After personally interviewing those who appear in this book on the record and scores of others anecdotally, it is clear that rainmakers share some very common characteristics that can all be acquired, rather than bred.

They get out of the classroom and learn from mentors.

They study the practice and its players.

They know at least one area very very well.

They supplement their knowledge with courses taught by bona fide experts.

They are bold. They act, rather than react. They envision, rather than see. They decide. They do. So, you can get out there and be bold or you can toil away in obscurity, second-guessing decisions. This is not like those commercials about sponsoring a child in Africa for pennies a day (which one of my subjects nobly did to great personal satisfaction); it is investing in yourself and the rest of your life. The current generation is always looking for a call to action, but misses it each time it is sounded. This is it. Get up. Get out. Get an umbrella.

On the last day of class, my torts professor told us that if we couldn't find satisfaction in the law, we just weren't looking hard enough. He encouraged us to look, listen and feel. He inspired us. Ten years later, I encourage you to do the same. The principles in this book are consistent with my professor's call to action. I was inspired. I am inspired. If that doesn't convince you, consider Rodney Glassman, winning a City Council seat while attending law school in Tucson, or Jill Dessalines retaining a Fortune 500 client in her 4th year, and the many others I had the good fortune to speak with.

Write an article, create a panel, start your own law review, run for office, have fun. Enjoy the law. Convey that enjoyment. Rinse. Repeat.

Chapter 2
Rainmakers Study for the Knowledge, Not the Grades

While much of success in the law is about academic performance, more of it is about interactive excellence. The level of success that creates happiness, satisfaction and genuine personal growth is only possible by learning who you are and how you can most effectively interact with others. It is those others who can provide guidance, support and ultimately, trust you enough to give you legal work.

This doesn't mean that you should not study. On the contrary, study often. The easier you can make the hard stuff, like getting a job before you even graduate, the harder you can try on the easy stuff, like meeting people, learning about business and finding your passion.

Studying is not always about reading a book or learning the difference between habit and character (a principle I could never quite figure out, hence my B- in Evidence). Sometimes it is about modeling behavior and learning how to hand someone your business card. It is about learning how to manage the butterflies before you walk into a room filled with strangers or call a professional contact for the first time. It is about beginning to understand people at their core (a worthy lifelong quest no doubt) and what transforms an individual from an ordinary professional into a rainmaker.

That transformation is often a slow brew. It is not necessarily a function of age since there are many prominent professionals in their thirties who are incredibly accomplished (some wunderkinds are even in their twenties), but of the processing necessary to realize the altered mindset. In an inherently risk-averse profession like the law, it takes tremendous fortitude to seek not only the acquisition of knowledge about a subject but pursue the understanding of its impact with equal vigor. It is through that understanding, however, that one can relate to those who are impacted. It allows you to stand in their shoes and share their perspective. It sets the foundation for a true relationship.

2.1 Get Out of the Classroom

Start by leaving your comfort zone. Prominent New York City employment attorney Stacey Gray spent much of her time immediately after graduation watching trials in Manhattan. "I showed up to so many cases that I got to know the usuals," says the founder of Stacey M. Gray P.C.

She met the reporters covering civil rights and the retirees looking for an entertaining way to spend their mornings. She engaged lawyers, paralegals and even judges in conversation. She learned the process and the protocol.

Students who learn how to practice even before they are permitted to do so have a tremendous advantage over their peers long after graduation.

2.1.1 AN INTERNSHIP CAN TRANSFORM YOUR ENTIRE CAREER

STUDENTS TAKE NOTE: You do not necessarily need to sit in on trials like Gray. You can take advantage of school-sanctioned internship programs and trial advocacy classes. While many law schools offer credit for these activities, some students avoid them because they are often graded on the pass/no-pass scale, rather than for a grade that will factor into their GPA.

They also fail to realize that relationships that are forged during internships can and generally do lead to business development activities later in practice. They even lead to job prospects during the pivotal period before graduation from law school.

While Ken Thompson, a founding partner with Thompson Wigdor & Gilly LLP in New York City, was at New York University School of Law in the early 1990s, he interned with Southern District Judge Robert P. Patterson, Jr. in lower Manhattan. That internship helped him secure a federal clerkship with United States District Judge Benjamin F. Gibson in the Western District of Michigan after graduation.

Also while at NYU, Thompson served as a research assistant for then-Professor Ronald K. Noble. When President Clinton nominated Noble to be the Undersecretary for Enforcement at the U.S. Department of Treasury, he asked Thompson to be his Special Assistant. Noble went on to become the Secretary General of Interpol, the international police organization based in Lyon, France, and Thompson spent five years as an Assistant U.S. Attorney in the Eastern District of New York. "In law school, the masses were running for the money, but I was running toward relationships," he says.

Those relationships have helped him build a successful litigation boutique over the past five years after developing a prominent reputation as a trial lawyer in the labor and employment group at Morgan, Lewis & Bockius. "Law students get caught up in the money, but if they just take time and are willing to be patient to get the money, it will come." Thompson encourages students to register for internships and participate in summer projects that will have a meaningful impact on their lives. "Doing so will plant seeds for a lifetime," he says.

The value of an internship or enrolling in a trial advocacy class is not just those seeds, but the opportunity they provide for them to grow. "If you want to become a trial attorney, you have to develop trial skills," says Gray. "You need to transition from the moot court argument that never happened, to navigating real life events that take place in court," she adds. When you do so, you start thinking and acting like an attorney who can actually provide counsel to people. You also start building relationships that can bear fruit in the future, whether one year or ten from that moment.

Law students and junior lawyers tend to see opportunities with tunnel vision by fulfilling the obligations of the internship with a satisfactory result, or completing the necessary research and then requesting an additional assignment. The successful interns strive for excellence rather than a satisfactory result because their mindset is to learn and accomplish as much as they can from the opportunity. They approach an internship as not only another chance to get the meaningful experience Gray recommends, but also to learn at a greater level of depth, which she and Thompson demonstrate.

My first client was a referral during my fourth year of practice from an attorney with whom I worked as an intern at a non-profit organization. There is absolutely no reason why your first client cannot come from a similar source even earlier in your career.

SIDEBAR: Beneficial Internships
- Learn why issues are important, rather than simply what issues are important.
- Listen to the answers people give, after they have answered the substantive question posed.
- Ask people about themselves, as well as about their work.
- Consider the factors that influence decision-making, as well as the decisions at issue.

- Work for free, but make sure you are getting value in terms of experience and perspective.
- Keep in touch with internship coordinators and colleagues as closely as you would with former employers and key professors.

Ben Gross is all about keeping in touch with professional contacts. He graduated with a JD/MBA from the University of Arizona in December of 2007 and was admittedly not at the top of his class. Like many people, especially students, he is not a fan of traditional networking. "I never know how to network because I never know what to say," he notes. He does, however, religiously maintain relationships with former employers and their networks.

Prior to law school, he worked full-time as the paralegal for an estate-planning attorney based in Tucson (home of the University of Arizona). Before that role, he was a computer specialist consulting on various projects. At the beginning of his first year, Ben called his boss once a month until one day the attorney asked him to join him and a friend for lunch. Ben mentioned that he is looking for a non-traditional job working on legal issues for a non-profit theater company. Two weeks later, he was on the phone with the president of the board of directors at the John F. Kennedy Center for the Performing Arts in Washington, D.C. "Opportunities have arisen just having conversations with people," he says.

Matthew Swaya is the Vice President and Assistant General Counsel of Litigation & Employment for Starbucks in Seattle, where he has been for a decade. He has a degree in industrial and labor relations from Cornell and attended Brooklyn Law School. "Go work for the government, judge or U.S. Attorney's office while in law school because there is nothing more valuable than seeing real work issues," he says. He had a clinical opportunity to sit with a state Supreme Court judge in the Bronx and shadow an assistant U.S. Attorney in Brooklyn. "Practical experience gives you a framework for the rest of your life," he adds.

The practical experience also provides the opportunity to test oneself and make mistakes. It provides a forum in which to ask questions that practitioners normally should not have. Most importantly, however, it builds the foundation for a lifetime of knowing others with a bright future. Judges become higher level judges, U.S. Attorneys become law firm partners and prominent government officials, among other professionals. As the career of a student blossoms, so too do the careers of all of those with whom that student had the opportunity to interact while in school or immediately upon graduation. These individuals form the core of a network, an advisory team and a prospective platform for client development.

2.1.2 BE A FLY ON THE WALL

Cathy Fleming, a partner with Nixon Peabody LLP and the Immediate Past President of the National Association of Women Lawyers, encourages students and junior associates to ask professors, partners and other supervisors to take them along on marketing events. "You can see how it is done and learn from people who are more experienced," she says. She learned early in her career that successful rainmakers think positively, which is a character trait that is not obvious or taught in school. She notes, "There is no downside unless you spill soup on someone at lunch."

In the same way that Swaya learned about professional practice through an internship, "it is helpful to watch other people who are skilled at rainmaking because you learn by example," says Andrea R. Clark, Senior Attorney for American Airlines in Dallas. Seeing how a seasoned lawyer pitches him or herself and the firm is invaluable, notes Clark.

Most people approach a prospective client meeting, or even an existing client meeting with the interest of solving the problem at issue. Those individuals want to learn the facts and circumstances behind an issue and dutifully research the rules to apply them to the information the client provided. The client, however, often wants to be heard as well. He or she wants counsel in addition to advice. Acknowledging that there is a problem that is personally impacting the client's representative can be as valuable as finding a solution. "There has to be a relationship between a client and the attorney first," says Clark. "Many law firm relationships are people-driven," she adds.

SIDEBAR: Law students and newly minted barristers can learn by watching.

- Notice physical mannerisms, eye contact, smiles, handshakes and gestures.
- Listen to follow-up questions and after the meeting, ask the person to whom you were listening why he or she asked one question over another.
- Observe note-taking techniques, if any. If the questioning lawyer took notes, ask what he or she recorded.

2.2 FORGET WHAT YOUR PROFESSORS SAY, DEVELOP EXPERTISE NOW

STUDENTS TAKE NOTE: Most practitioners spend three years of law school trying to think like lawyers and the rest of their lives trying not to. Students are taught to be generalists who can approach any topic with the same strategy and process. Once they start practicing, however, they realize that a small group of others who focused on a specialty have a distinct advantage. Take for example the one engineer that every student knows who has a job in a patent practice months before anyone else.

Adam Hemlock is a partner with Weil, Gotshal & Manges in New York City who focuses on antitrust and general IP licensing issues. Hemlock recommends that students pick a subject on which they would like to become an authority and hone their skills in that field. "The sooner in law school you can develop expertise in a particular area, the sooner you will be distinguishing yourself," says. Noting that the key to success is finding a narrow area, he highlights that "the era of the generalist is on the wane."

In the short term, leaving law school with a specialty makes you incredibly valuable to the firms that are interested in your expertise. Jeff Zigler graduated from New York Law School in May of 2007 with a job in healthcare consulting waiting for him. While studying, despite advice to the contrary, he focused on health issues, published on the topic and conveyed his interest in the area to prospective employers. The success of his strategy speaks for itself.

Like Zigler, one must build a reputation and the impression of knowledge in an area because it will, ironically, help you get the experience that you will need to get the expertise. "Once you have the threshold level of technical skill, it helps to build the perception of expertise to develop it more quickly," says attorney development expert Ross Fishman.

Fishman suggests that students create a website or blog on the subject in which they are interested. "The mere act of having the website gives the view of expertise to the visitor," he says. "If you didn't have the expertise you wouldn't have a website," he adds.

Although schools are not teaching students to hone these skills while they are living large on their student loans instead of in squalor repaying them, the savvy among them are starting to get the message. Websites, blogs, podcasts, vidcasts, wikis, social networking and others all offer unprecedented opportunities to find distinction before graduation. Most are even willing to do it, but are generally so busy scrambling to keep their heads above water academically that they don't make the time.

"I don't think it takes that long to develop real expertise," says William J. Toppeta, President of MetLife International. He notes that there are many areas in which the business community looks for a knowledgeable specialist in the law and elsewhere. "Often, you just don't find the precise subspecialty for which you are looking," he says.

Topetta recommends that students and new practitioners pick an area that they can master in an effort to build credibility very quickly. "The biggest message that I can send to younger generations is focus." An attorney himself, he highlights that "the ones who are most successful are the ones who do just a few things very well."

After law school, Toppeta recalls working hard and clocking long hours doing many different things. "I tried to make up for thinking by acting," he recalls. "Instead of taking the time to think through what I wanted to do, I spent time trying different things to see what I liked." If he could go back in time, Toppeta suggests that he would contemplate his areas of interest. "I tended to act too quickly without taking sufficient time to reflect," he notes. After six to seven years of practice, he eventually realized his passion for life insurance, health insurance and pension litigation. That passion ultimately led him to a remarkable level of success at the very top of one of the world's largest insurance companies.

Law students that realize their passion early by focusing on what interests them most will be more capable of conveying that enthusiasm.

Finding what you like is not quite like trying on a new pair of sneakers, but you get the point. The better it fits you, the faster you run (humor me).

SIDEBAR: Selecting a Specialty

- Talk to professors, clinic directors, employers and other professionals inside the law and out about how they decided to pursue their chosen careers.
- Listen to their answers and pay close attention to any silent regret.
- Start your research early—even first-years can talk to people (contrary to what your study group partners may tell you).
- Step outside of your comfort zone by opening your mind to areas and activities you had never before considered.

2.3 Continuing Legal Education is the Ideal Supplement for the Budding Expert

ASSOCIATES TAKE NOTE: There is no magic potion that one can drink to learn the mechanics of practicing law. Law school takes three years, and learning the ropes takes a lifetime. To help you on your journey, continuing legal education offers an ideal opportunity to learn not only the practical aspects of a practice area, but the highlights of what lawyers and their clients are most concerned with. "We get so focused on the bottom line that we forget there has to be a process of self-education," says Gray, who took almost 100 hours of CLE in 2004. "It was worth the investment because when someone starts talking about a conversation out of my expertise, I often understand the basics because I took a CLE on the subject," she says.

For lawyers, this effort helps with referrals and developing a conversational style on various topics. More importantly, however, the individuals that make presentations are excellent sources of information and guidance. In addition, use the CLE classroom time as an opportunity to meet people who are actually practicing in the area being discussed. The room will often be filled with in-house lawyers, law firm practitioners and government attorneys. In many states, every licensed practitioner is required to take continuing legal education and, therefore, it is the ideal environment in which to conduct your background research on the profession. Lawyers also have a special place in their hearts for others going through the rite of passage they all experienced.

SIDEBAR: How to Take Advantage of CLE Programs

- Sit in the middle of a row, rather than at the ends so that you can engage attendees in conversation.
- Try to register for courses that run more than one day so that you can return for follow-up the next day. Spending two days with someone tends to build a stronger relationship and offers additional opportunities to interact.
- Inquire about student rates or complimentary opportunities for attendance.
- Follow up with an e-mail to those presenters that spark your interest. Request an opportunity to have coffee, breakfast or lunch.
- Read the course materials. (Almost nobody actually does this.)

Consider that many full-day continuing legal education courses offer at least two breaks in the morning and two in the afternoon, as well as a lunch period. Use that time to find common ground with attendees. Fight the shy Larry David inside of you and strike up a conversation with your neighbor. You are both stuck in the audience; that predicament is a perfect segue.

Since you are already there, try to really learn the material. Instead of simply taking notes, list the take-away points from the program. Summarize each speaker's presentation into a few bullets. Not only will this help you learn the material, but it will make it much easier to engage your neighbor in conversation during the breaks.

2.4 Do as They Do: Follow Great Rainmakers and Their Techniques

One of the best things a law student or junior lawyer can do for himself or herself is find someone to emulate. This is not necessarily a mentor, but someone after whom he or she can model activities. This person doesn't have to be a lawyer, which is a conclusion that often seems to shock people. For purposes of self-promotion, sometimes looking outside the profession to obtain an insider's view is critical.

Continue asking people to have lunch with you. They may be lawyers you have met at a CLE class, or they could be family friends, or (my personal favorite) random individuals in whom you are generally interested that you contacted via cold call or unsolicited e-mail. You would be shocked at how generous seasoned professionals are with their time, particularly those who have achieved some level of success. They know that meeting you might offer them the same prospects as you meeting them. They also know that giving back by guiding the future of the profession is only positive.

"Start marketing on day one," says Julie Elgar, a senior associate with Ford & Harrison in Atlanta, Georgia and the author of the highly publicized "That's What She Said" blog. Elgar suggests that students and junior lawyers identify a rainmaker, or at least someone they find interesting, and invite them to lunch. Her first lunch of this type was helpful, and she notes that "everyone is willing to spend an hour to develop younger lawyers."

The key is to make the activity a routine. Find somewhere inexpensive but tasteful and prepare to treat (though most lawyers will often pick up the tab for a student or newbie saddled with $100,000 in postgraduate loans). "Take some time every week and try to see the forest for the trees," suggests Elgar.

A weekly plan is manageable and fits well into the schedule of a law student or newish associate. After all, you have to eat.

Sidebar: Meeting and Greeting
- Try to actually become a regular somewhere since your lunch partner may respect the special treatment.

- Know what you are ordering beforehand and make it simple. It is no time for the "When Harry Met Sally" routine.
- Conduct background research and prepare questions.
- Start carrying a small pocket-sized moleskin-type pad for notes. Whatever you bring, make sure it has some character.
- Wear a suit. Casual Friday or not, anything less is an insult.

As your lunch list develops, "make an effort to surround yourself with people who are on a success trajectory and try to grow with them," says Ira J. Coleman, managing partner of McDermott, Will & Emery's Miami office. This does not mean that students should only contact successful individuals. Rather, they should contact those people who have a spark in their eye that signals ambition and enthusiasm. Meeting with people who share excitement for their work with you makes for better conversation and more likely follow-up.

Be prepared to teach, as much as learn at these meetings. The person sitting across from the table may have questions as well. Answer them honestly, but not casually. The difference is that one makes you look genuine, the other makes you look like an amateur. Take a few minutes after each meeting to evaluate your behavior. Do not obsess over any misstatement or spilled drink, but identify areas of improvement and specifically work on them at the next meeting. Make notes of your conversation and opportunities for follow-up. For example, if the person you met is going to have an anniversary at their current job (let's say five years) in a few months, calendar that event and send him or her a congratulatory note. People appreciate those gestures—wouldn't you?

"Ultimately, it is a game of numbers," says Coleman. For that reason, he suggests that budding barristers keep their address books growing. More importantly, however, the search for the field that suits one most must continue. "Keep following up on industries that you like and that fascinate you," he adds. The point about picking something you like and focusing is because "it is hard to run parallel tracks on different things without diluting your personal brand," remarks Coleman.

Lawyers often wish they had more time to think of the direction they would like to take their career, as Toppeta often considered, but once they have their law school exit interview and realize the extent of their massive debt, they try to get a job. Then they spend years trying to keep it or find something better.

Students and those in the nascence of their career have the luxury of a clean slate. They can think before acting. Those who take that time end up more of a success. Period. The question is: Why are there so many others that don't give themselves a chance? Survey after survey shows that lawyers are dissatisfied for some reason, and by the time they realize their dissatisfaction, it is too late to change because they have been practicing too long and cannot muster the courage to make a move. Give yourself a little more time now so that you don't have to waste it later.

SIDEBAR: Managing Your Future in the Present
- Think before acting.
- Ask people about their mistakes and avoid repeating them.
- Take the time you need; there is no rush.

With stratospheric starting salaries and incredible pressure to bill, there are increased opportunities for lawyers like Elgar to be creative and take risks. "The traditional role of paying your dues and resting after partnership is over," says Coleman. "Everybody has to hustle," he adds.

The beauty of the hustle is that the more junior you are, the more choices you have in terms of the direction you get to take and the people with whom you have the chance to associate. "Keep moving until you have something that works for you," says Coleman. You don't have much time to find your true north, but you have enough to avoid getting lost along the way as long as you stay committed to the goal of self-sufficiency. "The billable hour you owe to the firm, the non-billable hour you owe to yourself," he remarks.

2.5 ASK FOR ADVICE

There is a fine line between following people around and becoming the paparazzi of the law school or bar. The key to successfully making connections with people is to demonstrate an honest interest in learning more about them. Asking direct questions is probably the best way to manifest this intent. "Younger people can easily seek advice from an older lawyer," says Warren Jackson, the Vice President and Associate General Counsel at DirecTV in southern California.

Once you meet someone (and the meeting does not turn out to be a disaster), consider follow-up opportunities. Do not bombard these individuals with spam-like e-mail, but certainly seek out their opinion when making important decisions on a first job, speaking at an event or relocating. "Most people enjoy that and are appreciative of it," adds Jackson.

SIDEBAR: Seeking Advice from an Advisory Board

- Use this resource sparingly to maximize its potency.
- Ask questions not only to learn the answers, but to also let the people you are asking know about your prospects and opportunities. If you are asking for assistance in deciding between an internship with the State Department and a summer associate position with an international law firm, the person you are asking will appreciate your interest in international legal matters without actually discussing it.
- Be selective about who you ask. By only asking certain individuals when you have a question, you can ask questions more frequently. You can also tailor a question to an individual's particular area of expertise, further demonstrating your knowledge of his or her background and experience.

Ultimately, "it is an art," says Jackson. It is in many ways like studying the great salespeople, adds Dennis Duffy, a partner with Baker Botts LLP in Houston and a former Vice President and Associate General Counsel for Time Warner Inc. "It is about bringing your authentic self and connecting with that person," he notes.

Duffy tells the story of a law student he once worked with who was the producer of corporate documentaries. The individual, now a lawyer in north Texas, is using his visual sense of trials and cases to great effect, Duffy notes. "It has enhanced his trial work because he has built the skill of visualization," he says. That ability of adding pictures to words gives him a unique perspective and helps him stand out.

That type of authentic self is not necessarily nurtured in law school, hence the ever-present conflict between practice and rainmaking. The very essence of what you need to succeed is stripped away by the pedagogical process. Taking steps (discussed in later chapters) to identify and hone these skills will lead to increased empowerment. It starts, however, by seeking knowledge from others. Asking for their advice is critical in learning from their good judgments and bad. Mistakes are a funny thing because while nobody wants to make them, they are often willing to share advice once they do. Seek out information on those learning experiences and incorporate them into your daily activities.

If Duffy recommends that law students and new lawyers study the great salespeople, then make your next breakfast or coffee with a salesperson that you admire and respect. You are not learning the law; you are learning how to stand out as a lawyer. For great technical skills, study the technicians. For great self-promotion tips, study those that promote for a living. The product may not matter since people do not buy things; they buy relationships with people who happen to sell things, whether they are services or widgets.

2.6 Start a Book Club

According to LexBlog's Kevin O'Keefe, "The only thing that will change you from the person you are today and the person you are five years from now is the impact on you of the books you read and people you meet." We already considered the possibilities for meeting people, but the reading portion of O'Keefe's advice seems a bit more daunting. Julia Cameron's *The Artist's Way* (Jeremy P. Tarcher/Putnam, 2002) is a great place to start. It offers exercises for expanding creative thinking and self-reflection.

The one characteristic of great rainmakers is to associate rainmaking activities with others. They bring colleagues to networking events to encourage and challenge. They also share successes and failures with contacts who are in their circles of trust.

Using this technique as a guide, consider starting a book club on the most useful and compelling topics and, of course, those related to self-enrichment and growth. By collaborating with others on a book club, one can build relationships while simultaneously learning from those thinkers that the rainmaking community, inside and outside of the law, considers the leaders.

In addition, by reading books that rainmakers read, there is a strong chance that the next time you meet with someone or ask a member of your advisory board for advice, he or she will have read the same book. Again, you will be perceived as someone that shares the same philosophy and set of values. It will also demonstrate that you are genuinely seeking answers to critical issues.

For general self-promotion principles, "any of the Seth Godin books are great," says Marco S. Nasca, Esq., a Chicago-based lawyer and the Regional Director for Iris Data Services. At the top of his list are *All Marketers are Liars* (Portfolio Hardcover, 2005) and *Purple Cow* (Penguin Books Ltd, 2005). Nasca also recommends that students subscribe to *Fast Company* magazine.

Reading about innovators and innovation is directly related to life in the law. These topics convey distinction in a tangible fashion and offer suggestions for modeling behavior and strategies.

Those looking for guidance on dealing with people, image-building, and developing mentors may want to pick up *The Critical 14 Years Of Your Professional Life* by Robert Dilenschneider (Citadel, 1998). "It is an excellent book on becoming a professional," says John E. Hellerman of Washington, D.C.-based Hellerman Baretz Communications LLC. "It's out of print but worth finding," he adds.

He also describes *Selling the Invisible* by Harry Beckwith (Texere, 2001) as "a marketing classic about selling intangible things like legal services and yourself." And, though much newer, he suggests that *Made to Stick* by Chip Heath and Dan Heath (Random House, 2007) is "sure to become a classic." The book addresses tactical communications such as persuasiveness and effective messaging.

Contrast the traditional with the non-traditional whenever possible. *Marketing Outrageously* by John Spoelstra (Bard Press, 2001) "is about thinking outside the box and not being afraid to take risks," says Jason Spitz, the Vice President of Marketing for World TeamTennis in New York City. "There's nothing wrong with the 4 P's they teach you in school as long as everyone else isn't doing the same thing," he adds.

You may want your book club to focus on a niche, such as career issues faced by women. *Women Don't Ask: Negotiation and the Gender Divide* by Linda Babcock & Sara Laschever (Princeton University Press, 2003) explains why women find it hard to ask for business, for raises, and other items, and offers advice on learning to do so, says Christine Baker, Vice President of Litigation for Realogy Corp. in Parsippany, N.J. and former commercial litigation partner with Drinker Biddle & Reath in Princeton, NJ. She was co-chair of her firm's Women's Initiative, a committee devoted to supporting women in their professional and personal lives and helping them succeed. She is also co-chair of the American Bar Association's Women Rainmakers committee.

Women face unique issues in the law. For that reason, *Women-at-Law: Lessons Learned Along the Pathways to Success* by Phyllis Horn Epstein (American Bar Association, 2004) is a great book for lawyers, particularly women, which includes helpful insight on legal career choices, says Julie Tower-Pierce, a self-described "mostly-at-home mother," attorney and professor at a military university, where she teaches cybercrime and cyberlaw. "I consider this a must-read especially for women lawyers because it tackles the difficult issue of work/family balance in the profession, and sets forth a number of practice possibilities that have worked for other lawyers, as revealed through the author's interviews of over 100 women lawyers," she adds.

A remarkable woman herself, famed blogger, lawyer and renaissance technophile, Newport Beach, California-based Denise Howell recommends: *The Cluetrain Manifesto: The End of Business as Usual* by Christopher Locke, Rick Levine, Doc Searls, and David Weinberger (Perseus Books Group, 2001); *Gonzo Marketing: Winning Through Worst Practices* by Christopher Locke (Perseus Books Group, 2002); *Small Pieces Loosely Joined: A Unified Theory of the Web* by David Weinberger (Perseus Books Group, 2003); and *The Long Tail: Why the Future of Business Is Selling Less of More* by Chris Anderson (Hyperion, 2006). "They all contain important insights for personal and business success in today's world," she says.

From the entrepreneurial perspective, read *Mavericks at Work: Why the Most Original Minds in Business Win* by William C. Taylor and Polly LaBarre (William Morrow, 2006), says Richard Demb, co-founder of Dale & Thomas Popcorn. Anyone getting started on a shoestring should read *Guerilla Marketing Weapons* by Jay Conrad Levinson (Plume, 1990), adds Sam Udani, Publisher of ILW.COM and Immigration Daily.

Books targeted at lawyers abound, but *How to Capture and Keep Clients: Marketing Strategies for Lawyers* edited by Jennifer J. Rose

(American Bar Association, 2006) gives practical ideas that you can implement immediately, says David J. Leffler of New York City's Leffler, McCaffrey & Marcus. In addition, the best books for professional services marketing are *True Professionalism* by David Maister (Free Press, 2000) and *Rainmaking Made Simple* by Mark Maraia (Professional Services Publishing, 2003), says Beverly Hedrick, the Director of Business Development at Nashville's Waller Lansden Dortch & Davis.

Still, more general books on life lessons have a deep impact on shaping the outlook for students and the lawyers they become. *Who Moved My Cheese?* by Spencer Johnson, MD (Vermilion, 2002) is a great book for young professionals because "if they learn early in life that success is not given to them—that they have to chase after it and find it—they will prepare themselves to tackle unanticipated professional challenges," says Michael C. Rakower, a commercial litigator in New York City and the recipient of the New York State Bar Association's 2006 Outstanding Young Lawyer Award. "Anyone considering starting his own law office should also read *How to Start and Build a Law Practice* by Jay G. Foonberg (American Bar Association, 2004)," adds the lawyer named in September of 2007 by Lawyers USA as one of eight in the nation on a "fast track to making a significant impact" on the legal profession.

Colleagues and clients may be reading slightly different books. One of the most popular is *Execution* by Larry Bossidy and Ram Charran (Crown Business, 2002). "It is the best treatment on how to get things done that I have seen," says Stephen Yelen, President and Founder of SRY Consult, Inc., a Long Island, New York-based Organizational Effectiveness firm. Yelen also recommends *Crucial Conversations* by Kerry Patterson, Joseph Grenney), et al. (McGraw-Hill, 2002), which he notes is "a terrific treatment of engagement and interaction." And, he adds that *The Velveteen Principles* by Toni Raiten-D'Antonio (HCI, 2006) is an interesting allegorical use of a children's story from which many of his clients have drawn different types of value.

From that same value perspective, Angelo Paparelli offers *The World is Flat* by Thomas Friedman (Picador, 2006) and *Good to Great* by Jim Collins (Collins, 2001). He also suggests that students (and practitioners for that matter) review *Eats Shoots & Leaves: Zero Tolerance Approach to Punctuation* by Lynne Truss (Gotham, 2006).

Paparelli's point is best demonstrated by the example of an attorney advertisement that appeared in a March 2007 state legal newspaper. In an announcement about a new law firm member, it highlighted that he focused on "white color defense." "In our rush to get the work out, we had better take the time to get the work right," says Rosalie Hamilton, author of *The Expert Witness Marketing Book* (Expert Communications, 2003) and Founder of Expert Communications.

In October of 2005, Andres Palacio read *The Namesake* by Jhumpa Lahiri (Mariner Books, 2004) and was inspired to start a book club in New York City. "I wanted to get a group of people together that was interested in multi-cultural literature," says Palacio, an assistant district attorney in his first year in Brooklyn.

The group now has five or six active members who meet monthly at a restaurant that corresponds to the book they are reading. There are also many periodic members on Palacio's mailing list, which includes doctors, bankers, lawyers, teachers, non-profit workers and others from diverse backgrounds. "I love reading the book and then discussing completely different takes on the literature," says Palacio. The club has read books that reveal the history, politics, and culture of many different groups. In addition, "the benefits of being in a book club include the possibility of meeting new people in this city and making contacts in a setting that is not as forced as a networking event," he adds.

He recommends starting with a few friends. "People really love to talk about literature and what it means to them," he notes. "We live in a busy society that doesn't make much room for this type of discussion so when people find an outlet to do so it is pleasantly surprising how receptive they can be."

He suggests posting information about your club on Craigslist.com and Readerscircle.org.

2.7 BE PATIENT

There is a great quote attributed to Sir Isaac Newton about patience from which law students (and perhaps the rest of us) can learn a great deal. "If I have made any valuable discoveries, it has been owing more to patient attention than to any other talent," Newton purportedly said. In other words, these things take time. Perhaps all those years, your grandmother was quoting Newton.

If there is one universal vice students share as a community, it is their loathing for waiting. They hate to wait for acceptance (or rejection) letters. The Law School Admission Council used to mail LSAT scores, but now e-mails them. It is probably more convenient for the Council, but certainly quicker for the candidate. And, so the culture of impatience is upon us. Next comes final exam grades, responses from employers, clerkships, bar results and the list goes on. "The payoff is often remote in terms of time and your marketing effort to stand out. It is something that has to be done every month, or even every week," says Jim Calloway, Director of the Oklahoma Bar Association's Management Assistance Program.

Action is the great antidote to impatience. When you are feeling anxious and concerned about a particular goal or challenge, do something toward that end. In the case of standing out, e-mail someone else, engage your book club or just write a thank you note (more on that later). Keep yourself in perpetual forward motion, but don't stress about instant gratification.

Remember that the process of building your future is similar to building your portfolio. You are taking steps to make life easier and more fulfilling some years down the road. It is unrealistic to expect dramatic changes. You are incorporating certain concepts into your lifestyle, rather than changing your life.

"The reality in-house is that if you are working in a large corporation and managing large litigation matters, you are generally not going to have a lot of work to give any one person in all geographic areas or in all areas of specialties," says Jill Dessalines, the Assistant General Counsel for McKesson Corporation in San Francisco. "If you make the right impression and you keep nurturing that relationship, you will get work, but not necessarily right away," she adds.

Students and junior lawyers have one great advantage over their more senior counterparts: They have almost no pressure to bring in business. As such, the people they call are not expecting any type of sales pitch. Ironically, because they have nothing to offer other than a genuine interest and sincerity, it is easier to build relationships with people who turn down most calls for coffee, lunch and, most certainly, advice. Harness the power of that innocuousness by reaching high and cultivating as many relationships as possible, but be patient and expect absolutely nothing in return. Nothing.

Leffler highlights that it takes time to become a really good lawyer and to build a network of people for business development purposes. "I had lunch with someone, came back to my office and nothing happened," he recalls of an earlier career experience. "If you want to really develop a relationship, it takes more than a long lunch," he says.

That relationship is often just an added bonus. The knowledge that one acquires and inspiration is often enough of a return that makes the investment worthwhile. Consider how much more interesting a day would be if it began with breakfast with the general counsel of a Fortune 500 company or the executive director of a prominent non-profit or a local politician. Anything is possible, but everything takes time.

SIDEBAR: Enhancing Patience

- Set reasonable expectations for the outcome of your efforts. If your goal is to simply learn something about and/ or from someone, you will always find success.
- Measure your return at the outset in terms of fulfillment, rather than tangible consequences, such as a job offer, new client or referral.
- Set a schedule for following up. If the person with whom you meet mentions an upcoming legal matter or event, add it to your calendar and wish them luck the day before. Make a habit of remembering key events in the lives of others. You will be remembered for remembering. People have large memories for the smallest of incidents.

Chapter 3
FIND A MENTOR

Until his third year, Michael Abramson, a recent graduate and former president of the Student Bar Association at The John Marshall Law School in Chicago never actually had to apply for a job. His mentor or networking contact always called ahead to recommend him for a position. "The legal profession is based on relationships," he says. "If you are not at a top tier law school or in the top 5%, you learn that you have to connect with people," he adds.

In the fall of 2004 (his first year), Abramson read an article about a local lawyer who was a competitive power lifter and was using the activity to raise money for the Chicago Bar Foundation's inner-city mentoring program. A power lifting national champion and the son of a world champion in the sport, Abramson hoped that he had found a guide for the legal career on which he had embarked.

That guide, Dan Cotter, the Assistant Vice President and Deputy General Counsel for Regulatory Affairs at the Argonaut Group, Inc., a publicly traded specialty insurance underwriter, listed his number at the end of the article and Abramson took the initiative of cold-calling him one day. The two started training together, and a remarkable mentoring relationship was formed—one that years later continues to benefit both individuals. Cotter has an award-winning training partner and Abramson had a successful practitioner (who is also an alumnus of John Marshall) to counsel him through the law school experience.

Abramson, now a practicing lawyer, highlights, "what has helped me the most is establishing a strong and genuine connection to my mentor." More importantly, he notes that Cotter is one of his best friends as well.

A mentor is a role model, says Lisa Linsky, a partner in the New York office of McDermott, Will & Emery LLP. It is someone who possesses professional and personal experience, and is willing to share it.

That may seem elusive to many, particularly in a profession in which so much is packed into so little time; however, it can be as easy as making a phone call like Abramson. Most lawyers are happy to provide guidance to students and younger lawyers. As a prosecutor for nearly two decades with the Westchester County District Attorney's office, Linsky mentored new assistant district attorneys, as well as law and college students who worked in the office.

A true mentor leads by example, she says. Successful mentors commit to helping their less experienced counterparts develop professionally and personally by providing guidance, support, constructive criticism and honesty.

Before picking up the receiver though, keep a few things in mind.

3.1 PRE-PLANNING

Create a game plan, suggests Cotter. For a mentoring relationship to be successful, the mentee must have a clearly defined sense of what he or she wants to achieve. And, that achievement should not, as a general rule, be to get a job. Abramson's goal was to connect with someone from whom he could learn and with whom he could share his own knowledge and experience.

Law students are often consumed by one, maybe two, concerns: to get a job and to pay off their student loans. Schools still typically instruct them to look at job listings and send resumes (and more resumes and more) in response. With the proliferation of websites that offer job listings, coaching and commiseration, students and new lawyers are fooled into believing that they are "job searching" and making progress based on the number of opportunities for which they apply. Those individuals rarely find what they are looking for, mostly because they have not yet defined what that is. "It is difficult to mentor people on career direction if they do not know where they are going," says Cotter.

He advises students and young associates to travel outside of their comfort zones and beyond the four walls of their offices to create a plan. A mentor can work with you on this process. To those who erroneously enlist the help of mentors when they are looking for something, Cotter advises that the time to start building a network and communicate with others in your field is before you need it. If you reach out to a mentor only when you want assistance, there is no genuine bond. Without the connection, there is little chance for either side to benefit from the relationship.

For Abramson and Cotter, the connection was power lifting and the law. For Robyn Goldstein, it was a mutual friend with whom she worked prior to entering law school. The 3L at the University of Houston

Law Center is the former ABA Representative and the Editor-in-Chief of the Houston Journal of International Law. She also spent four years prior to law school working in public interest and met a number of lawyers. During an interview for a sought-after summer position with a 500+ attorney firm in Houston, the interviewer and her former supervisor turned out to be best friends in law school. That common bond and her background led to an offer. "Every experience that you have in life is meaningful and cannot be taken for granted," she says. You never know which one someone else will relate to," she adds.

An active participant in his local bar association, Cotter encourages emerging lawyers to attend bar meetings and make every effort to meet people outside of their practice areas. "Hot areas of law become extinct rapidly so it doesn't hurt to get out and meet people beyond your specific practice area," he advises.

Sidebar: Mentorship Planning

- Clearly define your goals for the mentoring relationship.
- Travel outside of your comfort zone to create your plan.
- Start communicating with others before you need to.
- Don't take any experiences for granted.
- Make an effort to meet lawyers outside of your anticipated area of interest when you are still deciding.

3.2 Finding a Mentor

Most law schools around the country have some type of mentorship program. For example, Emory University Law School offers two types of formal mentoring programs. The first is called the Atlanta Mentor Program. With assistance from the school's alumni association, first and second-year students are paired with metro, Atlanta-based alumni according to practice interests. The second is the E*Mentor Program, which connects students with mentors located outside of metro Atlanta. This is especially useful for individuals who want to practice outside of the region or state. Correspondence takes place via e-mail and phone.

Some schools offer more specialized mentoring arrangements. The University of Chicago Law School, for example, offers first year female students the opportunity to participate in the Women's Mentoring Program and interact with female alumni. At Stanford Law School, the Public Interest Mentor Program connects first year students with faculty, alumni and more senior students with like interests. And, at the University of Michigan Law School, the International Student Mentor Program pairs second and third-year students with foreign LL.M. and exchange students. Pace University Law School offers a Minority Law Student Mentoring Program.

Schools with prominent mentoring programs include, among many others:

- Texas Tech University School of Law
- Southwestern Law School
- Washburn University School of Law
- George Washington University Law School
- Brooklyn Law School
- Loyola Law School
- University of Oregon School of Law
- New York Law School
- Ave Maria School of Law
- Widener University School of Law
- Boston College Law School
- Albany Law School
- The University of Tulsa College of Law

Bar associations of all sizes generally offer a program that pairs students and junior lawyers with experienced practitioners. Like those offered in law schools, these programs vary, but are often designed to enhance professionalism and civility among lawyers by catching people before they have been tainted. Their purpose is centered more on the character of the bar than the development of the student, but the end result is often the same—building relationships and molding character. Bar association programs also tend to offer exposure to expertise, rather than simply experience, which can be of value to students and new practitioners trying to select a field to pursue.

- Jacksonville Bar Association
- American Law Institute

- Hispanic Bar Association of Washington D.C.
- The Young Lawyers Section of the Chicago Bar Association
- Florida Bar Center for Professionalism
- Orange County Bar Association, Florida
- Maryland State Bar Association
- New Jersey Commission on Professionalism

By way of example, the Multnomah Bar Association, in Multnomah County in Portland, Oregon, has served attorneys in the community for a century. In 1980, it created the Young Lawyers Section for attorneys under 35 or those who have been practicing for fewer than five years. Young Lawyers Section members sign up and are paired with experienced practitioners with common interests based on applications submitted. The program technically runs from January through July of every year and encourages participants to interact at least monthly. "The idea is to help young lawyers with their practice-related questions," says John Belknap, a member of the Board of Directors of the Young Lawyers Section and liaison to the professionalism committee at the bar.

Belknap, an associate with Smith Freed & Eberhard in Portland, is serving as a mentor for the first time this year. "I expect to be answering all of the questions I had after my first year in law school," he notes. In addition to aiding the next generation of barristers, the mentoring relationship provides young lawyers with a few years of experience an opportunity to hone their infomercial and raise their individual profiles.

David I. Bean, an associate with Portland's Meyer & Wyse, applied for the Multnomah mentorship program in his first year of practice. The bar assigned a local divorce lawyer to be his mentor. Their relationship became so strong that a few years later, his mentor offered him a job. "A mentor can help you develop your career and answer questions that you wouldn't ask your boss," he says. "For me it led to a great job," he adds.

While in law school, Bean asked his mentor at the time, a local judge, to give him the names of three lawyers with whom he could meet. He continued the pattern by asking each of those lawyers for the names of three people. By the time he was done with law school, "I already knew half the lawyers in town," says Bean. "Most people only know the people they graduated from law school with because they haven't created the opportunity to meet other folks," he adds.

Bar associations offer an ideal environment for law students with no substantial prior work experience or lacking a national championship in a particular sport to meet like-minded practitioners.

If you are lucky, you may meet someone like Cotter or Linsky.

"One champion that sees your talent could change the course of your life," says Alex Wellen, an attorney, senior producer at CNN and the author of *Barman: Ping Pong, Pathos & Passing the Bar* (Three Rivers Press, 2004).

SIDEBAR: Connecting With a Mentor

- Most law schools and bar associations have some type of mentorship program.
- The mentoring relationship helps junior lawyers hone their presentation skills and enhance their profiles.
- Create opportunities to meet individuals outside of your ordinary circle of classmates and colleagues.

3.3 SEARCH FOR THE RIGHT FIT

You might also meet a role model like Tonya Grindon, the first woman to be promoted from associate to income partner in six years at Baker, Donelson, and to jump from income partner to equity partner in one. She mentors many young associates and notes that your mentor "has to be someone that you feel confident and comfortable to speak to."

Grindon notes that if your firm does not have a mentoring program established, you have to be proactive. Go to management and ask for one. The same is true for law students. If your school or local bar association lacks a structured program, follow the Michael Abramson model and find your own.

Successful mentoring relationships depend on regular meetings and open communication. Grindon takes her mentees to lunch monthly. "We download," she says. Your mentor should be interested in both your professional and personal concerns so that they can appropriately guide you.

"I view mentoring as part of my commitment to the firm or other workplace where I am employed," notes Linsky. "It extends outside of the workplace to others who may benefit from my experience and guidance," she adds.

"There is someone just like you out there," remarks Wellen. "It would be great to get to know him or her." Wellen's critically acclaimed memoir addresses law school issues, and he encourages students to spend time with mentors and ask them for thoughts and advice. "People are generally happy to find a mentee," he says.

3.4 The Authentic Mentoring Relationship

Mentoring programs are really only part of the battle. Once the program assigns a mentor to you, then what?

You should not view your mentor as the person that will get you a job, says Abramson. A mentor will teach you how to navigate law school and the legal profession, but you should not use him or her. In addition, you should not try to impress your mentor with your vast knowledge or unusual skills. "Be interested in what they are doing," he says. "Passion is magnetic."

If you are genuine and honest, a relationship will develop based on those characteristics. Bragging has the opposite effect of what people often intend. "Authenticity goes miles," adds Abramson. It makes people comfortable.

Ultimately, your enthusiasm and interest in someone else will define your connection. In Abramson's case, expressing interest in Cotter's power lifting was rewarded with invitations to dinners at charities for which Cotter was a board member. As a John Marshall student, he found himself at Chicago Bar Foundation events in an inflatable sumo suit with an attorney from Baker & McKenzie or challenging a partner from McDermott, Will & Emery on a mechanical bull. "The more people that are familiar with you, the greater chance of getting referred by someone and having it mean something," says Abramson.

While mentoring may seem like a function of serendipity rather than methodology, the right person needs to have your name at the right time. Abramson notes that law students, particularly those attending third and fourth tier schools, do not realize the importance of raising their visibility in the first year of law school. "You never know which of those connections will pay off," he highlights.

Students that pursue interests and demonstrate a genuine passion for those interests will connect more organically with a mentor or one who evolves into a mentor.

SIDEBAR: The Perfect Match

- Your mentor has to be someone with whom you feel comfortable speaking.
- Successful relationships depend on regular meetings and open communication.
- The more people familiar with you, the greater your chance of referrals to interesting opportunities.
- Mutual passions tend to connect more organically.

3.5 PRACTICAL TIPS FOR MENTEES

3.5.1 STUDY THE POOL OF MENTORS

Read legal websites like Law.com and Findlaw.com, or conduct detailed searches on the major search engines. These actions will give you an opportunity to learn about the professional interests of lawyers in your area or field. It will also help you identify those lawyers with whom you would like to speak and possibly secure as mentors.

For example, if you are considering healthcare work, search for articles on the topic, and narrow that list down to lawyers in your geographical area. Then select one or more of those lawyers with whom you share a connection. Obviously, if you went to the same college or law school, your entrée is an easy one. If, however, you have a less traditional commonality like power lifting or a pro bono interest in the arts, your reason for reaching out may be even stronger.

3.5.2 MAKE YOUR INITIAL CONTACT GENUINE

Law students and young lawyers often make the mistake of contacting prospective mentors with the intent of getting a job. Those who successfully navigate the mentoring process do so by seeking out guidance and insight, rather than direct assistance.

Your first e-mail or phone call should be brief. You should introduce yourself and ask for 15-minutes from your mentor-to-be. You might even want to suggest a meeting place, e.g., their office or a nearby Starbucks, to make the experience effortless for your prospect. They key is to make the meeting as easy as possible for the individual with whom you would like to meet seeking only to learn from this person's experience.

3.5.3 LEARN ABOUT YOUR MENTOR

Take the time to learn about your mentor. Conduct a Google search, review Martindale.com and visit his or her firm's website. Try to learn something about your mentor that will give you that ever-elusive connection or will at the very least impress him or her that you took the time to review his or her background.

The pros will ask a colleague, the receptionist or the person's secretary about something one may or may not know about the mentor. When asking in a genuine way and in anticipation of an initial meeting, most people related to your mentor will oblige with something (e.g., a favorite sports team or musical group, a bar membership or a volunteer activity).

3.5.4 CREATE OPPORTUNITIES TO INTERACT WITH YOUR MENTOR

Although the most dedicated mentors like Grindon and Linsky will follow up with their mentees and arrange regular meetings, it is really your responsibility to create reasons to meet. You probably do not want to invite your mentor to a house party, but if you have an extra theater ticket or know of a unique bar association event, he or she might appreciate an invitation. Not only do these gestures demonstrate your appreciation for his or her time, but they also create opportunities to strengthen the relationship that you share. You will also continue to learn from your mentor.

3.5.5 HONOR YOUR MENTOR

Your accomplishments reveal the guidance that your mentor has provided so share them with him or her. When you get your first job offer or an "A" in a class that you both discussed or win moot court, give a nod to your mentor.

In addition, if you are interviewing with a contact introduced to you by a mentor, be hypersensitive to the impression that you are making because it reflects not only on you, but on the judgment of your mentor as well. Be sure to characterize your relationship in a positive manner and report back on the experience.

3.5.6 REMEMBER YOUR MENTOR

Learn your mentor's birthday and any other dates of significance. If he or she has a wedding anniversary and it comes up in conversation, write it down. If he or she is up for partner, remember when and be sure to wish him or her luck. If he or she is arguing in court, closing a deal, or even buying a home, be thoughtful.

Thoughtfulness is the greatest tool that an unemployed law student or junior lawyer saddled with debt can use. There is no cost to sending an e-mail wishing someone luck, but it conveys a sense of attentiveness to the recipient. It demonstrates your ability to listen and to follow-up in a timely manner. The great lawyers remember things about their clients that exceed their clients' expectations. That and talent set them apart. It can do the same for you.

3.5.7 BE GRATEFUL

People just don't express gratitude enough. Perhaps it is a generational issue—today's law students may feel a greater sense of entitlement, particularly seeing starting salaries rising to $160,000 in major urban markets. Still, a "thank you" note goes a long way. In fact, you can almost never go wrong with one. It should be brief and perhaps via e-mail (for the CrackBerry addicted among us), but it should be sent and very soon after the event that prompted it.

Ben Gross enjoyed a guest lecture by a professor during his senior year in college so much that he sent him a short letter of appreciation. In response, that professor contacted him to ask if he could help prepare for an upcoming conference. When a lawyer in town later asked the professor for a referral to a student who could assist with his practice, he recommended Gross, who spent a year working full-time for that estate-planning attorney in Tucson before entering law school.

As his mentor, Ben's former employer asked him what he hopes to get out of the law school experience, rather than push him into a law firm. Although his friends questioned why he would take a position at the Kennedy Center during the summer of 2006 over a traditional legal employer, he notes "I practiced more law and had more meaningful interaction with people than any of my peers." It actually reaffirmed his conviction to practice in his own style. When he went looking for jobs during the summer of 2007, he reached out to the contacts he had made in Washington, D.C. "I spent all summer writing thank you notes and having coffee," recalls Gross. "I don't network because I am not good at it," he adds.

He admits that on paper, he is not competitive, but remarks that law students are too often dissuaded by their grades. He does not, however, expect to ever submit an application for a job. "I expect to be recommended for positions," he notes. People remember things about you when you express gratitude, he adds. "You end up on the right desk when you are recommended."

His practice of sending "thank you" notes has led to private lunches with professors, attorneys and other executives. "It is amazing how that small communication gets you in the door," says Gross who then remains in touch after his initial encounter.

Practically, Gross uses traditional Hallmark-type stationary on which he types a note (generally joking with the recipient about his penmanship). Whether you type or hand-write, reference individual conversations, advises Matthew Swaya of Starbucks. "Have the presence and the courage to say 'thanks for the opportunity and if you ever have anything for me, please think of me,'" he adds. Swaya recommends that law students and lawyers alike follow up and stay interested in the business and lives of those they meet. A referral for a babysitter or a contractor is almost as important on a day-to-day basis as a legal strategy for purposes of relationship-building.

You should also consider appropriate gifts that demonstrate appreciation. If your mentor likes guitars, perhaps a small book (under $10) on the subject is warranted. If your mentor drinks coffee, perhaps a gift card to Dunkin' Donuts is the right choice. Not only will these items help you build a relationship with your current mentor, but learning the practice of thoughtful gift-giving that does not bankrupt you will serve you well over the course of your career. Feel free to draw on your experience and background for items of this type. If you lived in the Far East and know of unique good luck charms, share your knowledge. If you have a background in American literature and think your mentor would appreciate a compilation of poetry, share it.

3.5.8 EXTEND YOURSELF TO YOUR MENTOR

If your mentor is working late on a project and could use some assistance, offer to help. Or, if she is working on something completely unrelated to the law, like planning a family event, offer to reach out to a contact on her behalf. People appreciate those who are willing to extend themselves with no expectation of a return. This is actually the great irony of serving others—although you are not looking for a reward and they know you are not expecting one, there is almost always a return for both parties involved.

Apply this philosophy on a regular basis because one of a student's greatest assets is his time, and one of a lawyer's most valuable commodities is hers. If you can alleviate some of the pressure on your mentor by freeing up some time, you have done a greater service than you can imagine.

This exercise will also help you understand what lawyers like your mentor value. Time is irreplaceable and precious, particularly for those who bill in tenths of an hour.

SIDEBAR: Successful Mentoring

- Study potential mentors.
- Seek guidance and insight, rather than assistance.
- Remember that your success reflects on your mentor.
- Be grateful for your mentor's support.
- Extend yourself to your mentor without any expectation of a return.

Chapter 4

THE SCIENCE OF SELF-PROMOTION: HOW A MARKETING COURSE CAN TRANSFORM YOUR FUTURE

I took Torts, Corporations, even Land Use in law school. For fun (and an easy grade), I took Client Counseling and Negotiations. For some actual good advice, I would have taken legal marketing, but it wasn't offered. In fact, it is almost never offered. That is, unless you are a student at Chicago-Kent College of Law in Chicago, IL or Valparaiso University School of Law in Valparaiso, IN. Those two schools have historically offered a free seminar (to students and alumni) on client development.

The program is generally given over eight one-hour lunchtime sessions in a four-week period during the summer. The course generally covers topics like networking, relationship-building and time management. Students that participate can apply for a $1,000 scholarship, offered by co-sponsors Nancy Roberts Linder and the Chicago Chapter of the Legal Marketing Association. Students compile all of the information gained during the program to create a hypothetical business plan, which requires them to prepare a networking list, consider the area of law they will practice, the type of firm setting they will be in, how to get clients and how to maintain relationships with those clients.

The course is designed based on discussions that Linder has had with law firms and assembled based on a model of giving law students discreet projects to outline and complete. "Students looking for a job have to learn how to market themselves," Linder says. Since marketing is very similar to looking for a job, the course provides the foundation for students to grow into lawyers that are adept at gaining visibility.

With a marketing and business administration degree earned *summa cum laude* from DePaul University, Muniza Bawaney, then a Chicago-Kent 1L, knew the value of having a competitive advantage and started thinking ahead. Recognizing the value of self-promotion, especially for law students, she enrolled in Linder's course. The scholarship was an added incentive.

The following fall, Bawaney's busy schedule did not allow her to interview with her top choice law firm through her school's on-campus interview program. A few sessions into Linder's seminar, however, Bawaney put her lessons to some good use. As luck would have it, and following the lecture on networking, Bawaney attended a local bar association meeting where she struck up a conversation with a lawyer who happened to work at her first choice law firm. "I would not normally have spoken to him," she says. Turns out, the lawyer submitted her resume and she received an offer to work as a summer associate. She is now a first year associate in that same office.

For law students who want to bring in clients and make it rain, a course teaches those basic principles necessary to make the trip easier: Study, promote yourself, network and enhance your visibility. And, as Bawaney did, create a plan.

4.1 LAW PRACTICE MANAGEMENT

STUDENTS TAKE NOTE: Thomas Jefferson School of Law in San Diego, Calif. introduced a new class in the fall of 2006 that teaches students how to build a practice and provides details concerning business decision-making and finances. It also offers programs on negotiation, but these are usually geared towards dispute resolution.

Bradley Corbett, a 3L at the school, took the new Law Practice Management course taught by a local criminal defense attorney. During the semester, Corbett learned how to obtain malpractice insurance, create the infrastructure for a functioning law office, the types of clients one should take, and ways to network. "It was a very practical class not just about substantive law but real world application," he says. For his final assignment, Corbett prepared a 3, 5, and 10-year plan.

Some of the more prominent programs around the country include "Law Office Management" at Quinnipiac University School of Law in Hamden, Conn. taught by Susan Cartier-Liebel, a solo practitioner in Northford, Conn.; "Introduction to Legal Practice" at Oklahoma City University School of Law taught by Professor Bill Conger; and, "The Business of Law" at Temple University's James E. Beasley School of Law in Philadelphia, Penn. According to recent news reports, Harvard Law School may even start a course in professional services in the spring of 2008.

Courses like these are starting to gain ground around the country because the American Bar Association is becoming more proactive in requiring law schools to expand their curriculum to include more skills courses, says Conger. "There is an argument about whether we are a business or a profession, which implies service and education," he notes. If we are going to do a service then we have to live up to certain enhancement of marketing strategies. Since we are saying who we are and what we stand for, it all relates to self-promotion.

That said, Conger's course and the others that are offered nationally do not focus specifically on marketing. Instead, it is just one component of a larger syllabus dedicated to teaching students how to start their own legal practice. Luckily for Corbett, his teacher spent a few classes discussing techniques like sending out holiday cards, advertising, and networking with possible referral sources. She also emphasized engaging in these activities with an ethical mindset so that law students and young lawyers develop effective practices that also comport with the standards of the profession.

That last point resonated strongly with Corbett, who is a member of the Church of Jesus Christ of Latter Day Saints and networks within that organization. "It is a way that I've got different connections," he says. Active in the J. Rubin Clark Law Society for Mormon lawyers, he attends dinner banquets and other functions to meet and speak with like-minded practitioners. Throughout San Diego's three law schools, Corbett notes that there are approximately 30-40 Mormon law students who interact regularly through the church. In fact, one of those students secured a job and needed to move. He recommended Corbett to replace him. "People aren't real big on selling their occupations in church but people know one another," he says. Of course, everyone knows that he is a law student interested in helping out.

Using some of the techniques that he learned in the course, Corbett has identified criminal defense work as his niche, but is hoping to practice personal injury and bankruptcy as well at the Pacific Law Center. He is planning to market himself by offering free consultations at a San Diego shelter, distributing flyers and local advertising.

4.2 CUSTOMIZED PROGRAMS

STUDENTS TAKE NOTE: Corbett's classmate, Alyssa McCorkle, also a 3L and the 2006-07 ABA Delegate at Thomas Jefferson, chose to enhance her marketing savvy by personally hosting programs at the school on networking and business etiquette. Her area of interest, international law, also required a different strategy given the complexity and barriers to entry inherent in the work.

She has organized her programs at Thomas Jefferson or in conjunction with the ABA in nearby locations. The school or the ABA covers all of the costs, while McCorkle benefits from the recognition as the coordinator. She also builds her reputation as a self-starter by repeatedly approaching the career services office or the dean for approval to host the events, which generally draw between 40 and 100 students. And, the response has been overwhelmingly positive. "All of the students thanked me for hosting these programs," she says. She spent an entire semester organizing three to four programs, with other students and the SBA assisting with the logistics. Now, other law schools have asked McCorkle to assist them with programs for their student body.

"Our school does not do enough with regards to networking so I have had to host programs myself," she says. Like most schools, Thomas Jefferson Law has a career services office that provides advice on resume preparation and career development, but that guidance is only available if you schedule an appointment. In collaboration with the ten other Southern California ABA-approved law schools, Thomas Jefferson School of Law cosponsors a series of regional career fairs that employers attend to meet prospective recruits.

To combat the lack of institutional support for business development training (and, of course, to encourage future membership), the San Diego County Bar Association offers a free membership to McCorkle and her classmates, as well as individuals attending the University of San Diego School of Law and California Western School of Law. The bar association creates student events and workshops on networking and related skills. Despite the coursework, her ability to create programs and bar association events, McCorkle is still frustrated with the lack of networking, etiquette, and business classes geared toward law students.

4.2.1 EXTERNAL RESOURCES

A regional chapter of the Business Marketing Association recently sponsored a program about media relations that teaches professionals how to promote their story to print, broadcast and online media. Programs like this one discuss pitching, public relations materials and press releases. They also teach you about maintaining contact with reporters so that you are quoted in the news. Not only do they teach media strategies for less than the cost of dinner in a major city ($25 for non-members), but you can ask questions of the speakers and view their PowerPoint presentations and related materials.

At another event across the country, the chapter featured the author of a prominent business book, as a speaker.

There are chapters in the following areas:

- Atlanta
- Boston
- Carolinas
- Chicago
- Colorado
- Dallas/Fort Worth
- Houston
- Hudson Valley
- Indianapolis
- Kansas City
- Milwaukee
- New Jersey
- New York City
- Northern California
- Pittsburgh
- Southern California
- St. Louis
- Tulsa

Some chapters have special memberships for students. Joining a marketing organization ensures that you will make contacts outside of the law who are interested in and skilled at marketing. You have the option of attending regular meetings, the annual and/or mid-year conferences, and/or intermittent programs like a webinar on public relations. Visit http://www.marketing.org/ to learn more.

Lexis and Westlaw also both offer free webinars, some of which cover marketing. Visit http://www.interaction.com/LNMH/go/webinars/archive.cfm to learn more.

Local bar associations will often offer a marketing course, or ten, that may be free or steeply discounted for student members. Not only are these courses a great source of guidance and insight, they serve as ideal networking opportunities to meet more senior lawyers with whom you might be able to collaborate on some novel business development strategy. Lawyers tend to welcome cheap (read: almost free) student assistance on projects that they cannot bill. Despite the visions you might have of smashing batteries in some remote foreign factory, this servitude, I mean training, could at a minimum get you the heck out of the library or your apartment or, at a maximum, help you build a deep relationship with an attorney in your area of practice and city.

SIDEBAR: Marketing Studies
- A marketing course teaches you how to promote yourself, network and enhance your visibility.
- They are becoming more popular because the ABA is encouraging law schools to offer more skills programming.
- Review webinars, teleseminars and books on marketing.

4.3 PRACTICAL APPLICATION

Alysia Kinsella, a Chicago-Kent alumna who attended Linder's program and won the scholarship notes, "since this course, I started keeping in better touch with my wider circle a little bit more for networking. If you touch base with people once or twice per year, you can better understand what is important to them."

The business of law is relationship-based and, therefore, self-promotion has to be crafted in a manner that considers the human side as well as the substantive legal issues. Since lawyers are close advisors to their clients, the trust and rapport factors are critical to the representation. Linder highlights "the lawyers that really get it use their network to connect people. It is the 'who knows who' thing."

Kinsella's greatest lesson in this course was that if you set goals that are too outrageous, like "a million dollars in business by second year," you are almost sure to fail or not even make the attempt. "People get discouraged and it is better to set lots of small manageable steps that you can accomplish, especially for a law student," she says. After Linder's course, she joined the ABA and the Chicago Bar Association.

With amorphous concepts like networking, advertising, ethics, client relations and communication capital thrown around in certain types of marketing courses, particularly those targeted at lawyers and law students, follow-up is often a challenge.

"The whole idea in trying to develop business is to find out what works for you and what you are capable of," says New York City-based marketing consultant, Arthur Levin of AGL Associates. Levin's starts with the premise that everyone is different and individuals need to identify those techniques that are successful on a regular basis.

4.3.1 BECOME A STORYTELLER

First, Levin recommends that law students understand what they are trying to sell and why anyone would want to buy it. "This is the main idea people truly don't understand."

For example, one shouldn't advise people that he is a real estate lawyer or a student with a particular skill set. Rather, try to convey what it is about you that will give others the confidence that you can help them in their hour of need. "You have to make a case to that person that you are fully capable, willing and able to take the significant problem from them and solve it," Levin says.

Demonstrate what you do by example. "The best way to do that is by telling illustrative stories," he notes. If you can offer visual and memorable examples of what you do and how you do it, the listener will carry your message forward for you all of the time. In the same way juries and the press remember one-liners from high-profile trials, interviewers and those with whom you network will remember your stories.

Start experimenting with your messaging now so that by the time these people are promoted up the chain of their respective careers, you are the person they think of as a problem-solver and trusted advisor. "The earlier you start, the more relationships you have when they count," adds Levin.

4.3.2 HELP OTHERS

It often sounds counterintuitive, but the best way to execute on marketing themes is to use them for the benefit of others first, then yourself. In fact, one of the best ways to get business is to give business as often as you can, highlights Levin. Commit yourself to meeting with professional friends and trying to help them gain recognition in their capacities at work. This helps to let others know what you do and how you do it. Most importantly, they come to like, trust and respect you. Law students have the added advantage of time. Imagine how popular you would be if you helped other lawyers in your community generate business or other students get their first job. Both tasks will make you one of the most memorable and appreciated individuals they will meet. Fast forward a few years (or sooner) and handsome dividends await for simply having a positive attitude and being somewhat selfless.

You do not even have to make them successful, just help them in the process. Start introducing friends to others who can provide important advice. Students and recent graduates are generally not personally connected to those people in a position to refer business to them. As such, there is no pressure. Rainmakers are always thinking about others and how to help those people at every opportunity. "Lawyers can't wait until they become a junior partner to think about business development, they need to start when they are in law school," urges Levin.

4.3.3 START WITH FRIENDS

Experiment with these methods on those with whom you socialize and feel comfortable in a natural environment. Those with whom you spend leisure time can be extremely good sources of job leads and potential business.

If you are just starting a family and spend all of your time at birthday parties and gymnastics classes, cultivate relationships with parents of your child's classmates. The key is to increase your circle of exposure as you become more adept at identifying who you are and how you can help others.

SIDEBAR: Making Marketing Personal

- Identify your individual marketing style.
- Start by targeting friends and seeking their constructive advice.
- Demonstrate what you do by example.
- Take an external marketing course.

4.4 JOIN THE LEGAL MARKETING ASSOCIATION

STUDENTS TAKE NOTE: In an effort to encourage law student participation, the Los Angeles chapter of the Legal Marketing Association started offering free memberships. Students are the future of legal marketing, says Cheryl Bame, a long-serving board member and former president of the LMA-LA chapter. "I don't know of any law school teaching law firm marketing, and most business schools do not teach it either," she adds.

To encourage participation in 2007, Bame, President of Bame Public Relations in Los Angeles, sent emails to professors at Los Angeles-area business and law schools. Like many, she believed that students would be better served if there were courses about law firm marketing and management in school since lawyers are required to be practitioners, marketers, and salespeople almost from day one.

Strangely, the response has been underwhelming but it is no surprise. Law students are a risk-averse group by nature and the Legal Marketing Association is a not-for-profit organization serving the entire community involved in marketing within the legal profession. Since marketing is not taught in law school, students are not often thinking of where to look for marketing opportunities. At $35/year, a student membership to the LMA is a good starting point, compared to the $350 for a full membership following graduation.

Some of the benefits include a discounted invitation to the annual conference and the opportunity to hear experts discuss trends and skill-building via webinar. There are also regional meetings and events that local chapters sponsor for networking and knowledge enhancement. Published works like Strategies magazine, white papers, surveys, and opinion papers are additional reasons to make contact. And, of course, access to the organization's membership directory, job bank and the LMA Listserv of over 2,000 subscribers are invaluable to those seeking resources for distinction.

The members of the LMA strive to enhance the level of understanding of marketing in the legal profession. Their careers are dedicated to the empowerment of attorneys and the advancement of law firms in the industry. Students who take the time to learn from them and receive some of their guidance will have a tremendous advantage over their peers when they begin practicing.

In the same way that Bame encouraged students to participate in the Los Angeles chapter of the LMA by offering free memberships, students should consider offering honorary practitioner memberships to student organizations. It gives the leadership of the organization a credible and honest reason to contact a practitioner, while also giving that lawyer the chance to meaningfully participate in the growth of a student-run group. If he or she is an alumnus of the school, the chances of success will be much higher so be selective in your efforts.

If, as Coleman says, there has been a shift in the way law firms hire and treat graduates, expecting them to have rainmaking potential earlier than historically required, then those who can demonstrate an interest and talent for the art are much more likely to get, keep and thrive in a job.

SIDEBAR: Legal Marketing 101

- Visit the LMA's website, http://www.legalmarketing.org.
- Review the chapter executives for your region and e-mail one or more individuals working at law firms on the list. Invite each to a cup of coffee to discuss the LMA and their work.
- Attend the next chapter breakfast or luncheon program.
- Simply ask people that you meet about the issues on which they are working. Those issues will be the very concepts that you need to master to hone your inner rainmaker.

Chapter 5
Networking & The Personal Aspects of Promoting Yourself

Someone once told me "network or not work," and that statement is more appropriate now than ever. With skyrocketing starting salaries at law firms and the competition growing to new heights, creative barristers in training are charting their own course one contact at a time.

Frank Seminerio is a 3L at Penn State's Dickinson School of Law. He is the school's representative to the ABA, which also gives him a seat on the executive board of Dickinson's student bar association. Serving as the liaison between students, the dean and faculty members at Penn State during the school's critical ABA accreditation period as it seeks to vault into the top tier of law schools in America has offered him extraordinary visibility. "These opportunities that I have had to speak with people and get my name out there internally and in the community have better prepared me to network in the future," he says.

Leadership positions in law school organizations present invaluable occasions to hone your interpersonal skills and time to master your 30-second self-marketing pitch. For example, ABA representatives have the unique good fortune of attending semi-annual and annual ABA meetings at which they meet with colleagues from around the country. "I am sure some time in the future, I will be able to leverage those contacts," Seminerio adds.

Student bar association presidents also get precious face time with community leaders and university administrators. Josh Moore was the first-ever repeat SBA President at the University of Detroit's Mercy School of Law. Not your traditional law student, Moore is 32, openly gay and has an adopted son. The soon-to-be solo defense lawyer describes his SBA Presidency as a blessing because it has afforded him the opportunity to meet judges before whom he hopes to practice, including justices on the Michigan Supreme Court. "I am not looking to get into your typical law firm because of my time constraints," he says. As a result of his clearly defined career goals, Moore has been leveraging his contacts.

A native of Detroit's inner city, he is marketing himself as a defense attorney who understands the needs of his community. "People are more likely to retain someone they know, they like and that they trust," Moore says. The 3L was a social worker coming into Mercy and has spent the past 4 years focusing on gay rights and children. At Mercy, he is a member of the Black Law Students Association, the Arab Chaldean Law Students Association (because Moore would like to reach out specifically to Arab Chaldeans in Dearborn, MI), and he is the president of the Gay Lesbian Straight Alliance. "My master plan is to help and be involved in the community at large," Moore says. Confident that his neighborhood ties will help him upon graduation, he notes, "there is something to be said about having a great network when you get out of law school."

The benefits of leadership aside, there can be only one SBA president and one ABA representative, so for the masses out there without one of these coveted titles, have no fear. Dan Cotter managed to master the art of networking without either of these positions. The Argonaut lawyer is an active mentor in the law student community and on the boards of directors for the Chicago Bar Association and the Chicago Bar Foundation. On those days when he is not traveling, Cotter will have lunch or coffee with someone in his network. "You have to be out there and keep networking," he advises. Not only is networking a good way to stay in touch with friends and colleagues, but the broader your network, the more likely you are to hear of things that are not public, he says. Those non-public matters might be a job opening or a client prospect, among others.

Cotter recommends that law students and young lawyers make at least four contacts per month with new or existing members of their networks. "What I often see are people who make random calls for contacts that might help them secure a new job. Even if you had someone's Rolodex, landing a job would be difficult." When you don't need anything, be a resource for other people so that it is a give-and-take.

For Cotter the method has worked. While he was a paralegal at CNA in law school, he sent thank you notes to his references for law school to tell them how he was doing and to simply update them. One of his references was the Treasurer at CNA. He had been trying to get to the law department for over two years. She called him to advise that she was friends with a senior attorney in the law department and would be happy to put in a recommendation. Although no jobs were open at the time, a paralegal left soon after and he was hired immediately.

Landing a "big firm" job at Lord, Bissell & Brook was also the result of a contact, though being number one in his evening law school class did not hurt. Despite his ranking, he was not having success getting interviews. His study partner happened to be a member of the Union League Club and sat on the insurance committee with a Lord, Bissell partner. Cotter had his friend introduce him to this partner, the two had lunch and voilà! Subsequent jobs at CNA, Unitrin and Argonaut were all the result of referrals from colleagues. "You never know what is out there," he says.

SIDEBAR: Networking Works

- Leadership positions in law school organizations help hone your interpersonal skills and master your 30-second self-marketing pitch.
- The broader your network, the more likely you are to hear of non-public opportunities.
- Making at least four new contacts per month is ideal.

5.1 THE THANK YOU METHOD

Cotter encourages people to remember the theory of networking through the following acronym: THANK YOU. They symbolize the gratefulness with which one should approach self-promotion.

5.1.1 TALK

To connect, you need to actually communicate with other human beings. The value of online chats, messaging and e-mail aside, communication should be in person or, at the very least, on the telephone. As a rule, in-person meetings are more valuable than those on the phone, and telephone conversations are more valuable than e-mail correspondence because the former reflects much more of who you are than the latter.

Prepare for your communication by doing a Google search on the individual you are meeting and spending a few minutes studying his or her background. Visit the website of his or her company or firm so that you have more insight into his or her work and background. Most importantly, study your own background. Be prepared to articulate the most important points about your history and future in 30 seconds. This is a great exercise for job interviews and potential client meetings.

Emulate the simple networking habits of those people that you would like to meet. For example, the lawyers and businesspeople you are trying to meet probably do not have a Facebook or MySpace page. They might, however, have a LinkedIn account, which is free, so open one yourself. You can network the same way the other sites allow except without the pictures of your "friends" at parties they (and possibly you) would rather forget.

Get to know the coffee shops and restaurants in your town or city. The iInternet and services like Citysearch.com help with this education. Your first offer should always be to meet at the office of the individual with whom you would like to network to make it as convenient for him as possible. If not at the office, be prepared to suggest a local meeting place nearby, even a Starbucks.

When suggesting the location, it should not be too expensive or too flashy. It should also not be too dirty or cheap. Always offer to pay (so bring money).

5.1.2 Handwritten Notes

Whenever possible, Cotter suggests that thank you notes be handwritten. Imagine how many e-mail messages you receive per day and triple it to try and comprehend how much junk you will get once you are out in the professional world for a while. On the flip side, the amount of snail mail has decreased dramatically so a handwritten note will certainly be noticed and appreciated (avoid the super hero stamps though). Stationary is not always cheap, but it is lower than your next student loan payment. Those who prepare in advance can put it on the holiday gift list. It makes a difference.

5.1.3 Appreciation

One of the worst things you can do when meeting someone for the first time is overstay your welcome. Sticking him or her with the bill or spilling coffee isn't great either, but I digress. Speaking of coffee, unless you have both decided to stay for lunch, never order a meal that will take time when the meeting was just for a hot drink. Also, avoid the nutty order for a venti half cap soy latte extra hot with one ice cube, a straw and low-fat cinnamon. It might lead to a chuckle or two, but you will forever be that person's Sally (as in "When Harry Met Sally") and certainly the subject of some office chatter at the end of a meeting. It won't kill you to get a plain old small (or "tall" depending on the shop) cup of joe for conversation purposes. The crazy orders also take more time, which violates the rule—be mindful of time and expect only 15 minutes or so during an initial meeting.

It also might not hurt to mention the time if you are there longer than 15-20 minutes so that your meeting partner knows that you are being mindful of the time. He or she will either thank you for the courtesy or let you know (if things are going well) that a few more minutes are available.

At this point, you should also review the mental itinerary of issues you wanted to make sure to discuss so that you don't miss anything.

5.1.4 News

If you remember that networking is much more about "them" than you, it will be successful every time. As such, think of reasons to genuinely make contact with members of your network. Cotter suggests finding articles of interest and mailing it to them. You should generally avoid articles about gossip and stick with practice development and related ideas (unless, of course, your relationship permits that level of informality).

To find such articles, you should pay close attention to local business and legal publications, such as your bar association magazine and trade magazines. In New York City, *Crain's New York Business* is an excellent source for inside details on market shifts that are often very interesting to lawyers in the area. *Crain's* lists promotions and career changes, as does *The New York Times* column "The Churn," and legal publications like the *National Law Journal* publicize large verdicts and other case-specific issues that might be of interest to your peers.

Much of this information can also be found on the Web, but again, avoid spamming those in your network with updates, since that effort will provide diminishing marginal returns after the first few. You should think of contact with this group as a scarce natural resource. You want every single engagement to be meaningful with no possibility of dilution because of overexposure.

Ultimately, if you find ways to use current news to enhance the work of those members of your network for whom that information may be valuable, they will appreciate your effort. That appreciation will build your relationship over the long term.

5.1.5 KEEP IN TOUCH

The perfect excuse for keeping in touch with a member of your network is to remember a milestone event in his or her life or career. A "happy birthday" e-mail still has meaning, just as much as "congratulations on making partner" or "great interview on CNN yesterday." People appreciate being remembered and acknowledged. This is a basic, yet incredibly underutilized principle of professional development.

Similarly, if you achieve something notable, let people know. For example, if you have had discussions about your first job with certain contacts and then receive an offer, let them know. When you pass the bar, send an e-mail.

Truly successful relationships are the result of honest and genuine cultivation over time. To that end, Cotter recommends that one make contact with 4 members of a network each week, either for lunch, coffee or a quick conversation. "It is necessary to keep the network strong," he says.

SIDEBAR: Thanks for Networking

- Communicate regularly with others inside and outside of your comfort zone.
- Follow-up with a handwritten note.
- Be mindful of the schedule of others.
- Find ways to make genuine contact with your network.
- Appreciate and acknowledge people for their efforts.

5.1.6 YOUR INNER CIRCLE

Networking becomes truly successful when it begins to overlap mentoring. It does so when the relationship advances to a level of trust such that members of your network become part of a team of trusted advisors. The team might consist of friends and family, but it should also feature more distant contacts on whose advice you can rely.

For Josh Moore, those connections have been valuable both from a professional and a business development standpoint. "It is very important to get someone who will be there when you come out, but who can teach you the ropes now," he says. "No amount of studying is going to take the place of human interaction," he adds.

5.1.7 OPTIMISM

When meeting people, be positive and enthusiastic. "People surround themselves with like-minded, interested individuals," says Angelo Paparelli. Students and young lawyers who can find a common bond with members of their network are much more likely to build a relationship over time, and this has a much higher probability of bearing fruit both personally and professionally.

That process only begins by understanding who you are, what you do and how lucky you are to be in that position. "There is no worse way to begin a conversation with someone than to be down on a current job position, the market in general, or other issues," says Cotter. Nobody wants to chat with a complainer. Perhaps you like an internship or are taking a fascinating course on international human rights. If so, focus on those aspects of the conversation. Save the sad stories and the gossip for your friends; network like you are the luckiest person in town.

The ultimate key is to network with your network's networks. How's that for a sentence? As Cotter notes, if you make positive first impressions on people, they will want to introduce you to others.

Start honing your skills by conducting a self-assessment. Make an actual list of your strengths, weaknesses, interests, likes and dislikes. Then select an area that has a business connection and consider the types of associations with which you might become involved.

Angelo Paparelli, for example, attends a number of varied theater productions to spark marketing and networking ideas. He also encourages involvement in organizations like The Center for Association Leadership, a group reportedly comprised of over 22,000 association CEOs, staff professionals, industry partners, and consultants. "We slice and dice in this country and in the world very finely," Paparelli says, indicating how niche-oriented our society has become. "Look at the associations that are out there and become an active member," he recommends.

Ultimately, the most successful networkers are adept at reaching outside of the legal profession as often as they can. To that end, Paparelli suggests that law students and junior lawyers think more about the world and less about the law. "You want to go beyond the idea of being a technician and become a trusted counselor," he says. "You learn this by mingling with your relationship capital," he adds.

A member of the National Speakers Association and the International Association of Business Communicators, Paparelli is constantly cultivating his skills of communication, advocacy, persuasion and influence. He suggests that those just entering the profession do the same. Doing so will keep you excited about what you are learning and how you can use that knowledge.

5.1.8 Unlimited Potential

The potential is remarkable. Imagine how much more fun law school would be if you spent time with people that offered inspiration as well as advice. Consider how exciting life would be if you had to choose between job offers, rather than hope for a response to an unsolicited resume. Most law students share the same hopes, fears and career goals. A few of them attempt to control their destinies by creating organic opportunities based on enthusiasm and excitement for the future (despite their massive debt). It takes a little effort and a strong memory to recall the words—Thank you.

Sidebar: Networking for YOU

- Networking becomes successful when it overlaps with mentoring.
- Be positive and enthusiastic as often as possible.
- The potential for effective networking is unlimited.

5.2 Networking for Non-Networkers

Taking the contrarian view, Nader Anise of Boca Raton, Fla.-based Nader Anise Lawyer Marketing says "networking could be a grand waste of time." Of course, Anise's point is that running between events collecting business cards is normally a useless exercise. It does not offer any advantage other than to consume one's schedule and provides only a false impression that you are doing something to expand your network.

While implementing Cotter's suggestions will help set the foundation for practice, professional and business development, Anise suggests walking down a less traditional path.

5.2.1 FORM AN ASSOCIATION

"This is one of the most successful covert strategies that is a clever method of getting your target market to approach you without really outwardly soliciting for clients," he says. When Williams Kastner's Galanda revived the Northwest Indian Bar Association in his first few years of practice, he did it out of a genuine interest to create a community of lawyers interested in Indian legal issues. Of course, the organization provided him with a platform to reach out to his members with press releases, at regular meetings and at community events. As his name became more recognized and his legal acumen more respected, his book of business grew exponentially.

Law students can benefit from this because many people they meet in law school will become clients and friends, says Anise. Forming an association allows you to better anticipate what they will become and enable you to form alliance earlier in their careers.

Local media will also begin associating you, as the founder of a particular organization, as an authority in the areas in which your group is involved. This recognition is certainly a conversation starter in a job interview, at a networking event and later, for client development. Starting an association demonstrates initiative, determination and commitment.

Anise cautions, however, that it cannot merely be perceived as a marketing vehicle. He provides the example of a personal injury lawyer that formed an association of injured motorcycle riders for the purpose of building a client base. While the association might provide valuable information to people injured on a motorcycle, it has to be independent of the work you do, but capable of furthering your mission.

Anise also highlights that "you need to have vision." "The smartest law student, the one who will have the most success, is the one who starts planning for his career and marketing initiatives while in law school," he says. Law students are fixated on getting a job and passing the bar, but if they look toward the horizon, those issues will seem secondary in comparison to their potential, he notes.

5.2.2 CREATE A DAY

STUDENTS TAKE NOTE: Anise recommends that law students start some sort of initiative like an "I love my lawyer day" (which he actually created and is celebrated annually) or "I hate exams day." It may sound unusual, but it will get noticed. The school paper will write about it, other students will certainly blog about it, and who knows? The local media may cover it and you may get a sponsor or two. Imagine a campus-wide party celebrating the universal disdain for legal tests.

Remember, the point of these ideas is not to actually make "I hate exams day" a national bank holiday. Rather, it is to begin honing your skills at self-promotion, aiding your development of a network and building name recognition.

For those of you less interested in silliness and more focused on actual community concerns, creating a breast cancer or AIDS awareness event, and even a program for Earth Day, can offer many of the same skills and benefits.

Ultimately, distinguishing yourself comes down to a combination of imagination, creativity and initiative.

Anise cites the example of a first-year at Nova Southeastern Law School in Fort Lauderdale who attempted to auction a seat in his constitutional law class to the highest bidder. Most classes aren't worth the eBay listing fee, but this student's offer reached $225 before he removed it. The reason: his professor was involved in the 2000 election dispute, among other high profile matters, and his class was incredibly popular. The student's name was everywhere in South Florida, which Anise believes could have put him ahead of the resume pile at every firm in the region.

Sidebar: Non-Networking

- Be creative in generating relationships and maintaining contact with others.
- Volunteer to assist others with their professional efforts.
- Create a day to celebrate something. Anything respectable will serve your purpose, which is simply to generate an opportunity to have fun and meet others.

Chapter 6
MAKE FRIENDS, NOT CONTACTS

In marketing, people develop contacts, leads and prospects. When planting seeds, people make friends. This book is about the latter, so connect. Use the "Thank You" method to engage and take the time to earn trust and establish genuine relationships. Cultivate those relationships over time and protect them well.

Start with those you have already met and have them introduce you to their friends, recommends Elizabeth "Betiayn" Tursi, the founder of Tursi Law Marketing Management. "I have gotten business from friends with whom I went to elementary school," she notes.

Identify true friends with judgment that you trust. Start with those you knew before law school and expect to know after graduation. For example, if you grew up in Kansas City and attend law school in Miami, ask your old friends from KC to introduce you to their friends in Miami and begin connecting with them in your newly adopted hometown.

Consider having a party the next time your mutual friend is in town. Write him or her a joint letter. Start a six degrees of your mutual friend running joke. That point of similarity can serve as the foundation for true organic growth. People want to connect with other people, but as they grow older and get more involved in their routines, it becomes harder. Asking friends to introduce you to their friends alleviates the burden.

There is also a greater chance that colleagues who know you will make an introduction that is consistent with your interests and ideologies. This will make it easier to find common ground and set the tone for sharing future experiences. A friend that knows about your interest in political activism will probably not introduce you to his or her favorite couch potato.

Like most of this process, however, there is an expectation of reciprocity, so be open to making introductions of those in your inner circle to others. After all, couch potatoes like to meet people too. Generously introducing friends and acquaintances to one another can be as valuable as meeting new individuals yourself.

Extending yourself and your clique to others is the first step in building a habit of being a giver rather than a taker. Givers are remembered for their selflessness, while takers are forgotten for their self-absorption. Be remembered.

Like other techniques, take the time to learn the art of introducing and meeting others because a failed personal relationship, like a blind date, could result in negative feedback. Follow up on this matchmaking and similarly let your friend know how the match he or she made is working out. The key is to remain gracious and appreciative of the efforts of others whatever the ultimate result. And, of course, always remember that the point of these relationships is to build friendships that will enrich your personal and professional experiences as you grow in your career. Looking for nothing more makes every contact honest and minimizes expectations.

Lawyers need to meet people to generate business. They need to network to retain clients. They need to generate name recognition to gain prominence. Law students and junior practitioners, on the other hand, need to learn the law. There is no pressure to meet people, retain clients or gain prominence. They can simply meet people for the enjoyment of connecting and learning about them to gain insight. That window of opportunity is short so take advantage of it while it is open.

SIDEBAR: Making Friends For a Reason

- Ask your close friends to introduce you to others in their trusted network with interests that are similar to yours.
- Consider friends that you might be able to connect.
- Develop opportunities to connect with others, either socially or professionally.
- Temper expectations to merely build relationships into friendships, rather than opportunities.

Argonaut's Cotter notes that you have to be out there and keep meeting others. "My advice is to be a resource for other people when you don't need anything so that it is a give-and-take." Despite the difficulty for students to grasp this concept, it is essential that they process Cotter's point.

I often describe this as the "Godfather" model of living. There is a great scene in the original film from 1972 where Don Corleone is speaking to an individual, asking him for a large favor for which he was willing to pay. Refusing to accept payment, Corleone explains "some day, and that day may never come, I will call upon you to do a service for me. But, until that day, accept this justice as a gift...." The relevance of that quote is not to cite one of my favorite movies (if I wanted to do that this book would be littered with quotes from "My Cousin Vinny"); no, it is to convey the idea that when you do for others, there is a natural and very sincere opportunity to call on them in the future. It is not for a return on your effort, but since you have already built up a certain level of credibility, people are more willing to entertain your request. It is a natural instinct. It is the essence of good relations. Be the person who says "it is my pleasure" or "good luck" first.

"Eventually your friends will land at a place from which you can get business," says Tursi. "It is all a matter of people contact," she adds. For that reason, Cotter suggests that students make at least four contacts per week. He often sees or hears of students calling people to randomly request job-searching assistance. "I can't recommend someone I don't know and whose resume I have never seen," he says. Seeking to take advantage of someone else's Rolodex is a pure waste of time.

Law students should start at the beginning. Discussing job prospects and learning about the job-hunting experiences of others is very different from calling and asking someone for help. Taking advice and guidance for consideration is the opposite of seeking it only as the means to an end, i.e., a job.

The interesting aspect of seeking guidance is that your questions will lead to answers, which will lead to a conversation that will inevitably turn to your own activities. There will be similarities in your job search or networking or academic experience that will often create a shared bond between you and the person with whom you are speaking. If you are authentic, that person will remember you. That memory could become invaluable if he or she hears of a job opening that may suit you.

6.1 Participate in Non-Legal Activities

The breadth of Cotter's network is considerable because he is a power lifter. He makes friends at lifting meets and has developed relationships with franchising and real estate executives with similar interests. "The key is to gain exposure to people that are outside of the profession," he says.

6.1.1 JOIN A SPORTS LEAGUE

Those successful in this regard simply follow their own roads. If they play tiddlywinks, they might join the International Federation of Tiddlywinks Associations. (Seriously, tiddlywinks has a worldwide following.) More conventional sports fans can engage their passion in intramural activities. Andy Hahn, a partner in the New York office of Seyfarth Shaw LLP formed a team when he was a junior associate at a prior firm. "A partner with whom I was working at the time wanted to create a firm volleyball squad, and I saw it as an opportunity to get to know him," says Hahn. That partner was the head of the litigation department of the prior firm. There are few meaningful ways to connect with more senior professionals, he notes. Hahn joined the team and practiced playing volleyball whenever possible. After the games, the partner in charge invited players to dinner and for cocktails. He later added Hahn to his litigation team and years later supported his partnership bid.

While Hahn's legal talent and dedication earned him the promotion, his interest in genuinely connecting with others was a strong supplement to his ability. In the same way that Cotter's mentee, Michael Abramson connected with Cotter through power lifting, Hahn connected through volleyball and other activities, including community service. Consider how you could connect with people. Whether through academics (though there has to be something more fun), politics or even unusual games made popular in the 19th century (like tiddlywinks), there is something that can connect you to someone in a different profession, stage of life or location. Julie Elgar, the author of *That's What She Said*, connects with people by blogging about her favorite television show.

Sports are probably the most popular and easiest activity in which to get involved. There are traditional teams like basketball and softball (and apparently volleyball), which are particularly common among law firm attorneys, and less common squads of people that bowl, run and swim. It is harder to get to know people under water, but you have to do what suits you (pun intended).

Arthur Levin had a client who played in a senior hockey league and made friends with his teammates. "There is a natural affinity to like-minded people," he says. When his teammates needed a lawyer, they asked Levin's client for advice. "People are more willing to give you work because you like what they like," he adds.

Athletics, in particular, bring out a certain level of enthusiasm that builds camaraderie and a healthy sense of competition. It also enhances shared memories and a culture of hopefulness. And, unlike most activities of this type, skill is not as important as heart. Since the point of connecting with people in this way is to demonstrate character, rather than performance, a sporting event provides an ideal forum in which to do so.

SIDEBAR: A Sporting Chance

- Join some type of group that is aligned with your interests. Sports are the most popular, but politics, academics and even something unusual like shopping might work. The point is to engage with others who are meaningfully committed to a similar activity.
- Identify opportunities to follow up when the principal activity is complete.
- Measure success by your level of interaction and personal satisfaction.
- Do not force yourself into an activity. Participate in events that are comfortable and naturally suited to who you are.

6.1.2 BECOME ACTIVE IN YOUR LOCAL CHAMBER OF COMMERCE

ASSOCIATES TAKE NOTE: Michele Rodon Carver is the Marketing Coordinator for Business Development at Lowndes, Drosdick, Doster, Kantor & Reed, P.A. in Orlando, Florida, and is a 2L at Florida A&M College of Law's sub-campus in Orlando. She was encouraged, and even inspired, to pursue a law degree by the partners with whom she works. She suggests that junior lawyers seek similar options for inspiration by engaging in activities with their local chambers of commerce.

For example, Leadership Orlando is a program sponsored by the Orlando Chamber of Commerce to foster community leadership among Central Floridians. Classes meet for nine different one-day sessions over an eight-month period. Each class, which falls on the first Thursday of each month from 7:30 a.m. to 5:00 p.m., examines a community-related theme. A new Leadership Orlando curriculum begins quarterly and Lowndes, Drosdick, Doster, Kantor & Reed generally registers one of its attorneys in each program. "It is one of the most rewarding things they have ever done," says Carver. She highlights that participants evaluate the public school system to consider reconciling environmental concerns with economic development and regional growth. "They are exposed to different industries and creative relationships with these people," she adds.

A program like this is probably more applicable to practicing lawyers, rather than students, given the $3,500 price tag for members of the Chamber of Commerce; however, students and young professionals have participated in the program, says Kathy Panter, the Vice President of Community Leadership for Leadership Orlando. "Most law firms in the region are members, as is the Florida A&M Law School," she adds.

Orlando is actually among a group of cities around the country that offers some type of local leadership program. They also exist in some form in Cleveland, Kansas City, Los Angeles, New York, Pittsburgh, San Francisco and St. Louis. "Leadership programs are a wonderful way to become connected in the community," says Panter.

There is generally a cost associated with participation, but you have to ask yourself whether it has a value equal to what you are spending. Those who enroll in these types of programs are often community leaders, business executives, politicians, and civic-minded individuals. At their core, they are simply interesting, knowledgeable and approachable people that share a common goal of local improvement. And, you get to spend eight months with a virtual who's who of your local community.

For instance, Alex Yaroslavsky, founder of the Yaro Group, a Manhattan-based employee relations firm, participated in Leadership New York from September of 2006 through May of 2007. He spent nine months working side-by-side with Gotham's political leaders, non-profit fundraisers, real estate developers, construction officials, investment bankers, municipal workers, and, of course, lawyers. There were 49 other people in his class.

Despite the $4,250 fee, "I would recommend it to others because there are so few opportunities to create a network of people with whom you are able to interact over a prolonged period of time," says Yaroslavsky. He notes that the program helps you learn about yourself, teaches you about leadership and provides insight about your home city. In Yaroslavsky's case, he became an expert on the Big Apple.

Students who are interested in programs of this type and are ineligible or unable to pay the fee or have it sponsored should still reach out to the local chamber of commerce for ideas on participating in events that provide similar experiences. Consider inviting alumni (either from the law school you attend or the college from where you graduated) that are participating in the program to come and speak to your student organization. Create a symposium on local issues and ask someone in this program to be a keynote speaker.

In fact, use the chamber of commerce and its programming as a springboard for ideas and seek the chamber's participation. Organizations often need an audience that will listen to its message and law students need a message to use as a means to build an audience. There is perfect synergy. This type of interaction is also well-suited to students who may have additional time and enthusiasm.

6.2 START WITH ALUMNI OF YOUR ALMA MATERS

STUDENTS TAKE NOTE: Law school students thinking about approaching the Chamber of Commerce should probably think first about leveraging their own chamber of college, that is, friends. "Part of having a strong network is staying in touch with people—so why not start with people with whom you have always wanted to stay in touch in the first place?" asks Hanson Bridgett rainmaking star Garner K. Weng. Noting that mid-level associates fail to think about the connection of their past to their future, "Friends from college or law school are people who hopefully already think well of you and can be just as likely as others to be able to connect you to business contacts," adds the San Francisco-based IP lawyer. For Weng, the key is simply starting by remaining connected to people with whom one has an existing relationship.

When he was a second- or third-year associate, he retained his first small client, but within a year or two, he built a larger base. His partnership election was one of the fastest in his firm's history and he soon became one of the youngest ever to chair a practice group and to serve on the firm's management committee.

While many junior lawyers do not see themselves at the same firm in five years, Weng encourages them to think of business development as planting seeds. "You plant a whole lot of them in different places—

and then you have to be patient." It is especially hard to know early on which efforts will prove the most fruitful; but if you are personally and professionally enriched while doing it, the end result should not be your primary goal in the early stages.

As Yaroslavsky mentioned, there are very few opportunities outside of the educational context to build meaningful histories with individuals. As one's career evolves and the time out of school expands, the ability to generate opportunities to work closely with those who could be business contacts a decade from now diminishes. Those lucky enough to participate in a leadership program like Yaroslavsky did in New York City can fight the trend, but ultimately, connections with law school and college friends set the foundation for a deeper relationship in the future.

"It starts in college, and once a college student recognizes that their next step is law school, start a content relationship database," recommends Tursi. This can be something as simple as formalizing your Microsoft Outlook address book, or a more sophisticated online e-mail marketing tool like Constant Contact. If you want to ultimately work with individuals with whom you have shared experiences and also like, starting with this group is essential. "You have to have a mindset that these are going to be the people that you want to deal with," Tursi adds.

6.2.1 GOING BACK PROPELS YOU FORWARD

STUDENTS TAKE NOTE: Lisa Landy had a high school friend working at the Australian Trade Commission in Miami, and when an importer needed a lawyer, her friend gave the company her number. She was in her second year of practice. The corporate partner in the Miami office of Akerman Senterfitt has since graduated to sophisticated multinational projects, but still maintains relationships with her high school colleagues as a result of that referral.

High school relationships were traditionally easier to cultivate for those remaining in the areas in which they were raised. The proliferation of technology, however, has helped today's law students and junior lawyers reach back more seamlessly. Services like Facebook and MySpace enable and enhance connections to high school friends and even beyond.

Consider how memories shape you. There is a genuine connection between people who attended high school together that is even more significant than those who share a college experience. Friends lose touch and they move away, but they generally do not forget. Since the goal is to begin developing significant links to people for the sole purpose of personal growth, reaching back to high school can be fruitful because the seeds you planted then have had much more time to sprout.

Tom Kane of LegalMarketingBlog.com tells a story of a partner at one of his firms who was riding the elevator in his building when a wealthy businessman entered the elevator after a meeting at another law firm in the same building. The businessman, who was looking for a lawyer to do his estate plan, recognized the lawyer, since he was tall and had played basketball at the high school they both attended more than three decades earlier. As a result of their conversation, the lawyer (who happened to be an estates lawyer) was retained—not because he graduated from Princeton and was Editor-in-Chief of his law review at The Ohio State University, but because they went to high school together. "The lesson is that you never know what contacts you make over the years will result in legal work," notes Kane. "It is best to not overlook, and lose touch with, those promising contacts you do make over the years," he adds.

Create a professional reunion function the next time you are in your hometown. Talk to the administration of your high school and ask if you can collaborate on an invitation-only alumni event to which select current high school students could also attend. By engaging the school, you incorporate an instant level of credibility and provide yourself with a platform from which to springboard. You get to be the person who coordinates the event and speaks with each alumnus. It is the ideal opportunity to connect. The people you are contacting see you as genuinely interested in celebrating their achievements, and the school views you as a supporter.

Christy Burke has mastered this idea. The 1993 graduate of Connecticut College and founder of Burke & Company, a New York City public relations and marketing firm, is the chairperson of the college's programming committee. To encourage alumni fundraising, she started the Distinguished Alumni Program. Her first honoree was the president of Forbes and she convinced the company to hold the event at the Forbes corporate headquarters in Manhattan. Twenty people attended. Her later programs have featured: Amy Gross, Editor-in-Chief of O Magazine;

Judy Licht Della Femina, network news correspondent and Full Frontal Fashion producer; Sally Susman, Executive VP for Global Communications for Estée Lauder; and Ted Chapin, President and Executive Director of the Rogers and Hammerstein Organization. "It has been incredibly rewarding from the standpoint of how engaging it is to hear alumni success stories," Burke says. "Even if someone is not in the exact same field, there are universally applicable principles," she adds.

This regular interaction can lead to new ideas and opportunities. At the Forbes event, Burke conceived of a Connecticut College Entrepreneurs Forum to support the efforts of fellow alumni launching businesses. Her first event was a panel of alumni entrepreneurs moderated by a branding expert, whom she asked to be a co-founder of the series.

All of Burke's events take place on a quarterly basis over lunch for 1½ hours. There is a 45-minute question and answer session with the distinguished alumnus of the school, who Burke has the privilege of interviewing in front of her peers. "For people right out of school, it is great because they are looking to make their first contact," she says.

Since the model is low wear and tear on the alumni office, the events are relatively easy to set up, notes Burke. And, there can be multiple events taking place in multiple cities. From a momentum standpoint, it builds on itself. In addition to recommendations from the alumni office, which suggests potential guests, trustees of the college will also share ideas with her.

Once each program is finalized, the college distributes an e-mail to its entire list of alumni and Burke's name appears on every single one. Today, people she has not met will call her to let her know that they cannot attend the event but will ask her about her services. "The bottom line is that you don't have to piggy back on existing events; you can create your own," she notes.

Burke's efforts demonstrate that you can create programs that build relationships on a shoestring budget where you are essentially the producer, creator and co-star. "Everybody wins," she says.

You could even tailor this type of activity to alumni with experience in the law and law-related industries, or to business leaders in a specific industry, such as technology or aerospace. The possibilities are virtually unlimited and simply require imagination.

SIDEBAR: Leveraging Alumni Relations

- Read the alumni magazine from your college and law school.
- Research online sources of information, such as Facebook and MySpace.
- Consider creating alumni events and other creative programming sponsored by your alma mater.

6.2.2 HELP ALUMNI HELP EACH OTHER

There is a lawyer in the Midwest who has lunch or dinner with an alumnus of his law school every time he is in a new city. He asks each person he meets for a short bio and incorporates it into an alumni reference book. He started this practice early in his career because he felt that junior lawyers could have a greater impact sharing relationships with more senior lawyers with whom they work

The book is a relatively simple idea, but "simple ideas can be great ones," observes Roy Ginsburg, an attorney and business development coach in Minneapolis. "Alumni want to help other alumni," he adds.

Like Burke's featured alumni programs, the reference book gives the creator the opportunity to meet individuals nationwide that he otherwise would not have the chance to meet. A law student can accomplish this task as easily as a practitioner with 30 years of experience. Of course, the law student has the added advantage of free time (after studying, stressing over studying and lamenting the need to study, of course).

Since students (and junior lawyers for that matter) don't get to travel that much, consider arranging telephone interviews and encouraging participation via e-mail. Technology-savvy individuals might want to take this reference book into the current generation and create an online version so that participants can draft, modify and update their biographies at their convenience.

In the same way that Burke has the weight of the college behind her and is mentioned in official e-mail messages about her events, the creator of an alumni guide could have the school host the item online and associate himself or herself with it as the editor. Given the amount of traffic that an institution receives, it will likely propel the editor to the top of the search engine rankings in a very positive and noteworthy manner.

As you learn about fellow alumni, consider ways to connect those in similar or complementary industries. This will have no direct benefit to your efforts, but will build the perception that you care about others and take a genuine interest in their work. If your matchmaking is successful, people start to realize that you listen and hear.

Since most people simply want to be heard, that reputation will serve you well. It will build trust among your peers. That trust over time will lead to unforeseen and unpredictable prospects.

To further promote the project, consider inviting alumni to round-table discussions where you serve as the moderator, similar to Burke's role as the interviewer. These discussions could be endorsed and publicized by the school. They will serve to encourage participation in the alumni guidebook, but also create additional chances to meet interesting people.

As for timing, the projects get done when you can get to them. There is absolutely no pressure for you to perform at a certain time or to fulfill a preset commitment. The remarkable aspect of this strategy is that it truly is all benefit. School officials can support many of the details with representatives of the alumni with whom you are in contact.

You simply build your frame of reference and conduct additional planting in the garden of your future. "The most successful lawyers tend to know the most people," advises Ginsburg. "It is a question of just getting to know them when you can so that you feel comfortable following up," he adds.

SIDEBAR: Guiding Alumni

- Contact alumni that you know and ask for a short bio. Assemble them into a very short packet.
- Forward this packet to the alumni relations office of your alma mater and offer it as an example of a possible alumni connection.
- Consider which alumni you would personally like to meet because the experience, while only minimally time-consuming, should be something on which you would like to focus.

If you see this as an opportunity to assist others, rather than your-self, it will be much more rewarding. Naturally, that assistance will be returned to you. "At its core, the process is about helping each other out," says Ginsburg.

Chapter 7
FINDING CREATIVE WAYS TO CONNECT

Not everyone has a positive view of his or her high school, and sometimes college, years. For those people, the alumni approach may not be ideal. That said, I would offer that from a probability standpoint, there has to be someone from your alma mater with whom you would like to connect, but never had the chance to meet. If you are still unconvinced, there are a number of ways to reach out that do not have anything to do with where you went to school.

They incorporate some of the universal characteristics of great rainmakers, which are collaboration and strategic thinking. They are also generally creative and foster an ability to think differently.

The key to any venture of this type is that it be low maintenance. It has to be manageable within your schedule, whether that is a schedule of classes or cases. Students tend to have more flexibility, but the will to engage is a function of interest and availability. Build these activities around your habits and style. Otherwise, the entire exercise is a waste of time.

7.1 JOIN A TOASTMASTERS CLUB

Alumni activities tend to work because there is a sense of comradeship. You went to the same school with someone else, had that same annoying professor or lived in the same dorm. There is history. You worked toward the same goal: earning a degree.

The best relationship-building activities are those that require an honest effort and a willingness to be openly judged. This is similar to some of the sports justifications cited above. For Thom Singer, joining Toastmasters was the best business decision he made in his career. The Austin-based expert in branding, positioning and networking is the author of two books and was a semi-finalist in the 2002 Toastmasters International World Championship of Public Speaking, making him among the top 20 Toastmasters of 20,000 who competed that year.

By way of background, Toastmasters International launched its first club in 1924. Today, there are approximately 10,500 clubs and more than 200,000 members in about 90 countries.

A typical club is made up of 20 to 30 people who meet regularly (weekly or bi-weekly) for about an hour. Their purpose, according to the organization's website, is to help participants "learn the arts of speaking, listening and thinking—vital skills that promote self-actualization, enhance leadership, foster human understanding and contribute to the betterment of mankind."

For law students and junior lawyers just starting to repay their student loans, the price of admission ($54 per year—$27 every six months with a $20 new member fee) and the potential opportunities for connecting with people (Toastmasters counts among its members a former Miss America, congressmen, astronauts and athletes) are unparalleled. The obligation is probably about two hours per month depending on the club you join, and the 20-30 people that you meet are generally committed for the long term. That commitment extends from their success to yours. It is part of the organization's culture. In the process you will become a better and more comfortable public speaker.

SIDEBAR: Getting a Taste of Toastmasters
- Visit www.Toastmasters.org and find a local chapter.
- Call the chapter representative listed online and ask if you can attend as a guest.
- Seek advice on participation from someone on your personal advisory board. With 200,000 members, someone you know must know a Toastmasters member.

7.1.1 CREATE A BREAKFAST, LUNCH OR DINNER CLUB

Among his many other accomplishments, Dr. Rodney Glassman (who has a PhD. in arid land resource sciences) graduated with a J.D. in December of 2007 from the University of Arizona. While in school, he created the South of 45 Breakfast Club in Tucson to provide a forum for community involvement and political awareness consisting of up-and-coming business professionals, ultimately to benefit the community and agencies dedicated to serving children.

The club meets on the second Friday of each month from 6:45-8:00am at a local restaurant. Meetings regularly feature local political figures and host a non-profit agency serving children that educates the group on their programs. Following that presentation, South of 45 awards a $500 donation.

Membership is limited to individuals under 45 and the fee is $360 per year ($180 of which is tax deductible). The program has become so popular that "many law firms proactively send associates to become members," says Glassman. In fact, when he appears at law school networking events, junior associates are eager to introduce him to the partners.

By artfully weaving a networking event with a community interest, Glassman has created a virtual lock on success. It requires no promotion because the donations generate good will and the prospects among the members lead to annual growth. "Getting involved in the community is the cheapest type of advertising because it is tax deductible," says Glassman.

Dan Cotter had a similar idea. He and a classmate from law school created the "TM Network" soon after their graduation. Their goal for "The Monthly Network" was to bring one person outside of the law to lunch for an intimate foursome. At the end of the year, the duo would invite all the participants from the TM Network to a single gathering. "The nice thing was that once per month, you were networking," says Cotter. After two and a half years, they ceased operating the lunch series on a regular basis but amassed a contact list of over 100 individuals with whom they remain in touch.

Programs similar to those created by Glassman and Cotter are successful because they serve as events, rather than efforts. We schedule events and postpone efforts at self-improvement even though we know they have significant potential. Also, associating empowerment with an actual meal gives the essential act of nourishment multiple points of value. After all, everyone has to eat.

I once interviewed a successful partner at a large law firm over lunch and asked him how he was able to generate such a diverse portfolio of clients. His answer: "I never eat alone." This partner had made a concerted effort to eat with someone every single meal. That does not mean that the experience requires formality; it simply should be shared.

SIDEBAR: Meetings and Mealtime
- Review your schedule and determine which meal works best for you.

- Breakfast and lunch tend to be easier to schedule than dinner for professional events, though dinner is often a more social experience.
- Identify a local restaurant with which to partner.
- Develop a strategy for inviting guests and other potential participants.
- Make it convenient.

One other interesting point about food-oriented events is that they can be the subjects of local news coverage. The art of mastering time management to accomplish multiple goals simultaneously is an almost mythical topic in the business community. Law students can hone this technique to the point of success before they even take the bar exam.

For those who are conscious about budgeting, meals do not have to be expensive. In fact, you can start with a brown bag lunch where those that join you bring a snack. You might eventually be able to gravitate to a local sandwich shop. Then, like Glassman, you can charge a fee and collaborate with a restaurant to offer a meeting place and a discount.

Before meeting with anyone, you should conduct some background research. It could be as simple as asking another contact about the individual or a slightly more involved Google query. It is not quite a job interview, but you are taking someone's valuable time, and demonstrating even a modest amount of preparation will convey your appreciation. It will also fill any initially awkward silence since you will know about the individual and can speak about his or her interests.

7.1.2 MEET LAW FIRM MARKETING REPRESENTATIVES

Law students and junior lawyers interested in making friends with people who know how to make friends should look no further than law firm marketing representatives. Most mid-sized and large firms have dedicated business development groups that teach lawyers about themselves through training, and about the firm through marketing. These groups also generate material to share with clients and prospective clients.

"It helps if a law student can cozy up to the marketing folks," says Nancy Manzo, a Seattle-based Practice Director in Marketing Solutions with Hubbard One (owned by the parent company of the publisher of this book), who for many years was an independent consultant on using technology to enhance marketing and served as the Director of Business Development for an AmLaw 100 law firm. Those in the marketing department can help guide a student on selecting an association to join, recommending key contacts and adding his or her name to the firm's mailing lists, she advises. That last factor is key because it may lead to invitations to firm-sponsored seminars and events.

Manzo's suggestion may be easier said than done. Unlike lawyers, whose contact information can be found throughout the Internet, in the phonebook and on the law firm's website, business development, marketing and other individuals serving in a non-legal capacity (though may themselves be lawyers) are not often listed publicly.

Have no fear, the information is not that difficult to obtain. If you have a law firm in mind, simply call its main number and ask the receptionist for the chief marketing officer. You might also be able to find the contact for this individual online, if he or she is with a higher-profile organization. The Legal Marketing Association may be able to help with this research, particularly if you are interested in a specific firm or group of firms. It can, however, be a bit of a wild goose chase.

Those seeking to streamline the process should consider utilizing the *Law Firms Yellow Book*, published semi-annually by Leadership Directories. Unlike other industry resources, this is a directory of law firm leaders and is not limited to those who are practicing. It has the title, educational background, address, phone number and e-mail address for over 21,000 managing attorneys and administrators at over 700 law firms (some even include pictures), which Leadership Directories staff members verify for accuracy.

At $319 for an annual subscription shipped in two separate volumes (winter and summer), the cost is steep for students and most associates, but there is value beyond the numbers. Listings like these could help job seekers connect with lawyers and law firm administrators that share the same educational background and career path. For example, if an attorney has experience with the Consumer Product Safety Commission, which is less common than other government agencies, and you have an interest in that type of work, your request for coffee or lunch is more likely to be accepted. The *Yellow Book* has indices for practice areas (with over 100 categories and sub-specialties), law schools (listed alphabetically and chronologically by graduation dates) and geographic location (e.g., state, city and even locality). If you choose not to buy a personal copy, it is probably available in your law school or firm library. If not, suggest that they purchase a copy and feel free to use my points about the advantages.

The purpose of a guide like the *Law Firms Yellow Book* is to organize and diversify your efforts. While initially meeting random individuals is part of the process, setting forth a strategy for how to spend your time and where to focus your effort will help you develop a reputation in a field or within a specific community. For example, if you get to know a number of law firm marketing professionals in your city, your name is more likely to come up in conversation for one reason or another. When someone shares something about you with someone else without knowing that you are a mutual acquaintance, you have achieved a milestone.

The goal is to become known as someone that truly takes an interest in others and the insight they offer. It is also to follow up on those efforts with tangible activities like meetings and invitations to interesting programs whenever possible.

Sidebar: Seeking Internal Law Firm Guidance

- Take a look at the *Law Firms Yellow Book*.
- Select law firms that you would like to target for further investigation. Don't sell yourself short during this selection process. Regardless of your law school or your grades, reach as high as you would like. Feel free to contact the marketing director for the biggest law firm in your city, even if that city is Manhattan, Chicago or Los Angeles.
- Find some connection to the marketing executive that you contact before e-mailing or calling. They are talented and busy, but usually generous with their time. Give them an honest reason to meet you.

7.2 Stay in Touch

Whatever way you choose to make friends, the key is to stay in touch with them. The modern trend is to do this primarily by e-mail. Whichever way you choose, be consistent and be effective. "There is no particular course that one ought to take, but it is more of having a curious mind about a client's business or about the business development process," says Dennis Duffy at Baker Botts and also the former General Counsel for the University of Houston.

Some people are responsive to instant messages and others find it very intrusive. There are those that do not read mass e-mails and many who send certain phone calls to voicemail. Try to identify the method that works best for you and for your audience. Each method, including snail mail, has its appropriate occasion and your goal will be to experiment until you match them.

Law school is a microcosm of relationship-building in that there is a diverse population working toward a common goal with distinct needs, values and interests. In the same way that you communicate with fellow students, stay in touch with people that you meet (and with whom you hope to become friends) by following up on problems that they discuss. Make an honest effort to understand their concerns so that you can try to help. In addition, try to comprehend their business and industry. "Express an interest in what others care about even if you don't understand it," adds Duffy.

There is an intuitive, even silent, process occurring behind the scenes. Those best suited to planting seeds are individuals who manifest their interest in others. "The mistake that lawyers make is to see business development methods as a secret," he adds.

7.2.1 REMEMBER BIRTHDAYS

The key to success in following up is using practical tools to do the hard work, which is essentially remembering everything about everyone. Start with birthdays because they are simple. A short note wishing someone a good day ("I was thinking of you and wanted to wish you a very happy birthday"—feel free to copy this verbatim if you happen to get writer's block) is always effective. It clearly indicates that someone is important enough for you to take a moment out of your day to wish them well. E-mail is probably best for this. It is non-intrusive and will almost always elicit some type of response.

There are specialty services, such as BirthdayAlarm.com that help keep track of certain occasions, but you can probably just use a calendar.

Those associated with your e-mail are often the best because they send reminders directly to your inbox according to your settings. Remembering the birthday is actually the easy part. Learning the date is much harder.

For some lawyers, the Martindale-Hubbell directory may list the birthday on their practice profiles. For others, you might be able to find their birthdates online via the Birth Database (www.birthdatabase.com). As striking as the site sounds, it is free and actually contains a list of 120 million names and birthdates legitimately taken from public records. For those that do not appear in the Birth Database, you will simply have to ask or note it down if it comes up in conversation.

You have a genuine opportunity to distinguish yourself with a short note for this occasion. It is an ideal chance to stay connected, but could turn out to be a mistake if improperly used. Remember to proofread your message. You do not want to give the impression that while thoughtful, you are careless. In addition, avoid electronic greeting cards unless you are truly friends with the person to whom you are sending the message. They are unprofessional and recipients will frequently mistake them for spam.

The question of whether to send an actual card remains an open one. Although thank you notes are often sent in traditional form, birthday cards in the professional context may seem somewhat misplaced. That is a judgment call for you as the sender. In general, however, avoid complicating your contact. The point is to let someone know that you remembered something about him or her and want to genuinely offer your best wishes. Period.

SIDEBAR: Happy Birthday to You

- Check Martindale-Hubbell or the Birth Database for birthdates.
- Add the date to your calendar and set it for an automatic reminder on the day of the event. Avoid multiple reminders, as they will serve to confuse you. Similarly, do not set them too far in advance as erroneously sending an e-mail the day or two before the actual birthday will reduce the potency of your effort.
- Draft a simple message that can be sent by e-mail. If pos-

sible, reference a recent meeting or conversation with the recipient.

- Try not to use this message as an opportunity to promote your activities. Such an effort will detract from the genuine nature of the note.

7.2.2 Use an Electronic Calendar

Those using paper-based calendar systems must upgrade as their efforts to stay connected evolve because the volume will be too difficult to process alone. Outlook and most online tools are sufficient for this purpose. If you have a Google Gmail account, then use Google Calendar. If you have a Yahoo Mail account, then use Yahoo Calendar. Given the similarities in functionality, the purpose is to become accustomed to the use of the instrument, rather than obsess over its selection.

In addition to having a better memory than you, the digital calendar is constantly checking for events throughout the day, whereas you may only check your date book in the morning. Like all calendars, those found online are only as good as the information you provide. If you do not tell the system that a contact's birthday is on a certain date, it will not remind you. As such, each time an event is mentioned in conversation or noted in an e-mail, quickly record it in your calendar. Also, your information is accessible from anywhere you can connect to the Internet (which includes your BlackBerry, and if you are that cool, your iPhone). It can also be shared and you can even program the system to forward reminders to your mobile phone and multiple e-mail accounts.

Forgetting dates that are important to others is a rookie mistake that you should eliminate from your character as early in your career as possible. You will be surprised how much more important it becomes for you to remember important events as you adapt to the custom.

There are social benefits to this as well. No more phone calls from your parents chastising you for missing your grandmother's birthday or apologies to your significant other for forgetting to ask about a job interview or, worse, planning for an anniversary.

Take it slow and work out the kinks. Like most of the techniques discussed in this book, there is no rush. You have the time, so use it.

Sidebar: Modern Calendaring

- Explore the calendar program associated with your e-mail service.
- Begin experimenting by setting reminders for upcoming events and have them sent to various e-mail accounts and your mobile phone.
- When planning to follow up with people, set specific dates and times for those efforts. Add them to your calendar.

7.2.3 Compile a Mailing List

I am not sure how effective holiday cards are for purposes of standing out because they are often lost in the shuffle of the yuletide paper chase. Some people send Thanskgiving or New Year's cards instead. Others tailor the cards for their particular industry. For example, a realtor might send cards during the spring market.

For law students and junior lawyers, the act of sending the cards is not as important as preparing to send them. Ultimately, the entire ordeal of distributing holiday cards is valuable for only one reason: the mailing list. Making the list requires a review of your entire inventory of contacts. It also requires constant modification and evaluation.

It is, however, flawed because holiday cards are generally the only piece of correspondence that is sent by regular mail anymore. End-of-the-year mailing lists do not typically include e-mail addresses, which tend to be the communication method of choice. As such, take the time to make two lists: one for mailing and another for everything else. You can enter them into the address book associated with your e-mail account and then export them as necessary. While maintaining a list in the form of a word processing document is sufficient, those that keep contact details in a dynamically updated format tend to be able to make updates more quickly and seamlessly.

Some website hosting packages include simple mailing list programs. In addition, there are services, such as Constant Contact, that offer advanced tools for as little as $15/month depending on how many people you plan to include. More sophisticated tools let you know how many people read your e-mail, how long they spent and other key details. Whatever you choose, make it easy and portable. In addition, back it up often.

There is a natural reluctance to use a mailing list to broadcast your activities to others, but most people actually want to hear from you. In fact, they will be rooting for you, especially if they know you as a result of your efforts to inquire about them and their work. That said, use your list sparingly. Do not send messages about the level of difficulty of your final exams or the frustrations you are having with a job search. If you receive a Corpus Juris Secundum award or make law review, definitely let them know. Similarly, if you pass the bar, win your first case or achieve some other milestone, convey it to the group.

The mailing list is helpful for you to reach a large group simultaneously, but it is also useful for gauging how well you are achieving the goals that you set for yourself. In fact, mention in your e-mails plans that you have for the future. If you will be running for student bar association president or ABA representative, let everyone know. When you achieve that milestone, you will have another organic reason to be in touch.

Lists of this type are also helpful for new associates at firms because they help demonstrate to the firm's leadership that you are thinking about your future and that of the partnership. Doing so helps you develop an internal market for your services since the more senior lawyers are your first clients. "You want to display some fire in the belly," says Duffy. He notes that in most cases a firm decides whether a junior lawyer will be promoted to the partnership after his or her first three or four years. "They ask whether you are thinking like a partner and about the broader interest of the firm rather than your own personal perspective," he adds. Developing a mailing list is a tangible means of displaying your effort. But, again, guard its use closely to maximize its value and potential return.

Sidebar: The Basics of Mailing Lists
- Start compiling e-mail addresses of your contacts.
- Incorporate them into a unified program that allows simple modification.
- Use the tools sparingly and carefully evaluate the opportunities for distribution.

7.2.4 IF YOU INVITE THEM, THEY MIGHT COME

The value of a mailing list is significant, but only if the substance of what is sent has meaning to those you are trying to reach. Oklahoma City's Professor Conger suggests that law students and junior lawyers incorporate invitations to self-created events as part of this practice. He recommends that after spending about six months cultivating your advisory board, create an event and invite those on your list. For new practitioners, a law firm would be an appropriate forum for this event. Law students may be able to use, with school approval, clinic facilities or student activity areas. Serve light hors d'oeuvres and beverages, Conger advises.

These events serve to give you the chance to engage in person, but to also find opportunities to connect with others in a way that will offer future follow-up opportunities. Conger cautions that one lawyer he knew held an open house and nobody came.

Be prepared to give people a tour of what you do and why. Two of Conger's former students purchased a building in Oklahoma City's art district that looks like a small elementary school. These types of venues are ideal for open houses and internal events. They can convey a message about who the hosts are, how they practice law and their creative approach.

You may also want to seek sponsors for your event to defray any potential cost and to give an appearance of credibility. For example, perhaps a company that is involved with legal education or the legal community in some way might have an interest in providing refreshments at your event. This not only makes your life easier, but also gets you into the habit of collaborating on events of this type. If the event is well attended, that company may also be interested in working together again.

SIDEBAR: Open Houses

- Target local members of your network for a casual event.
- Select the venue carefully, as it will convey a message about you personally and professionally.
- Consider soliciting the assistance of a vendor to help defray the cost and lend credibility.

7.3 MAKING CONVERSATION

Many people fear that once they have an opportunity to actually meet with someone of interest, they will have absolutely nothing worth talking about. For students this is especially common. After all, the general counsel of a Fortune 500 company may not necessarily be interested in discussing your MySpace page or how stressed out you might be. He or she will want to get to know you though, so there must be a compromise drawn between how you feel and how you present yourself.

When meeting with someone, "understand the business, understand what they do and understand the public hot issues," says American Airlines' Clark. She recommends that students and junior attorneys study the media and understand what the media is reporting about current events impacting your meeting partner's industry or business.

On that note, "it is important to be intellectually charged," says DirecTV's Jackson. Novels, magazines, movies and even television are items that drive conversation. The law rarely does, unless you are discussing something political (which could backfire). Art, literature, sports, music, etc. give you the tools to make small talk. "You need to appear learned because that ultimately is what this profession is about," says Jackson. "It is more than just talking law all the time because it is a given that you will be up on what is in your field," he adds.

Aggregating news services, RSS feeds, interesting blogs and industry-specific websites are all useful sources of information prior to meeting with someone new. As I mentioned earlier, conduct a search on this individual as well in case something new has occurred since you last spoke. It is much more powerful to begin a conversation by congratulating someone on an event that just took place, rather than have him or her share that information with you.

But be prepared to talk about yourself, says Clark. You should also have interesting details about your school or firm, and basic facts, such as the size, clinics and/or practice groups, and the work that you do on a daily basis. I have never figured out why, but the most random questions seem to come up in conversation. When was your firm founded? How many students were in your second year class? What is the bar passage rate from your school or in your state? What is the composition of your practice group from a diversity perspective?

More importantly, remember to mention the interesting aspects of your background that may not appear on your resume, such as your love of cooking or the children's book you may be writing. "To be interesting is more interesting," says Jackson.

For law students who are concerned that they do not know enough of the law or issues facing lawyers, heed Jackson's advice. Be professional, but also be yourself. Be the breath of fresh air that people are hoping for when they answer your call to meet. Remember, most professionals are bombarded with meeting requests from salespeople in one form or another. This could even be a partner contacting the general counsel of a company for which he or she works. Law students and junior attorneys by extension are virtually immune from that compromised view. Since you can only offer genuine conversation and honest perspective, there is no concern on the part of the person with whom you are trying to meet that your intent is anything but sincere. Being yourself helps to support that impression.

Of course, as I mentioned above, some conversation topics may not only turn out to be uncomfortable, but could ruin a relationship that you have not yet even developed. Avoid political discussions, unless you know that you share the same views. Also, don't discuss money, private health matters, or personal relationship issues. To some this may sound silly, but there are many who accidentally start down a path on one of these topics and extricating themselves from it becomes so complicated that there is no viable means of return to the universe of acceptable discussion. Naturally, these are only guidelines and you will have to use your judgment as to how well this strategy works.

From a conversational tone perspective, excise immature and casually offensive words from your vocabulary. There are many newly admitted lawyers who still speak as if they are in college, and many law students who don't give this enough thought. If the effort you put forth in law school toward meeting people and developing relationships is an investment in your future, invest wisely with your best effort. The last thing you want is to describe something in a colloquial manner and for the recipient of the comment to take it offensively.

"I am always surprised by how many people are not prepared to speak in a conversational way about what they do," says Clark. She notes that many people are not comfortable talking about themselves and their businesses or firms. "The legal profession is very relationship-driven because one always wants to work with a lawyer who can do the work who she really likes," she adds.

Do not assume, however, that just because you have a conversation with someone, there will be immediate follow-up or some tangible benefit. The purpose is to experiment, to learn how to carry yourself, and to grow into the profession. That initial conversation also provides students with the opportunity to keep their names in front of that individual. Students and new lawyers could send legal updates to their contacts whenever available.

Google Alerts are free email updates of the most current Web, news, and/or blog results from the search engine's database. You can use them to follow an issue of importance to a friend, or something less professional but equally as important to him or her. This could include a film, sports event or local issue. You can set the search terms and frequency with which you would like a response.

SIDEBAR: Making Conversation
- Research the background and interests of the person with whom you are speaking before meeting. Use RSS feeds and blogs to educate yourself on popular culture as well as legal and corporate matters of professional interest.
- Specifically avoid certain topics of conversation that may create discomfort.
- Experiment with Google Alerts and similar services that allow you to follow issues of significance.

7.3.1 WHAT IF I AM UNCOMFORTABLE IN SOCIAL SITUATIONS?
It is easy to advise someone to simply get acquainted with others. Yet even with strict instructions and a simplified plan of action, there are those who feel awkward in cold-call originated conversations. Many lawyers do not appear in court, take depositions or speak publicly because of similar fears. These fears are activated long before one becomes a first-year and linger long after he or she makes partner.

"Shyness and nervousness can be addressed," says David Leffler, a corporate lawyer who represents technology clients, women-owned businesses and other entrepreneurial and growing companies. The founder of Leffler Marcus & McCaffrey LLC notes that law students must face this obstacle and overcome it early in their careers.

The type of engagement with others discussed in this section is an ideal opportunity to conquer the demons. They offer a safe environment in which to experiment in awkward social situations. If you find yourself concerned about your demeanor, use these meetings as an opportunity to hone your skills and overcome your apprehension.

For instance, those who feel ill at ease in bar association networking events can attend regular student events to acclimate themselves to similar programs. In addition, during meetings with members of your advisory board, you may want to share your perceived weakness with the person to whom you are speaking. You can then ask for suggestions for improvement in those areas.

While you do not want to convey a complete inability to interact, a desire to improve and enhance your communications skills is always respected. The irony of self-improvement is that when one openly admits to a limitation, it strengthens his or her ability to convey honesty. There is something very genuine about overcoming a flaw and asking for assistance to do so. If all else fails, "you can get a coach," Leffler advises.

Leffler advises that most professionals make mistakes in their careers. "They go out there a few times, feel like miserable failures and realize that something has to change," he says. He recommends practice in one form or another. "It is worth the time to do that because you will get tools for the rest of your life in your professional career," he adds.

Once you are practicing full-time and worried about generating business, making partner or managing the normal stress of life, self-improvement will be less of a priority. Making it an essential element of your goals now will allow more time to focus on urgent matters later. In addition, one significant, but shorter-term benefit of this process will be to hone your interviewing skills. As you increase the frequency with which you befriend members of the legal and business community, you will not only become more comfortable with your presentation skills, but you will more clearly define your personal description and self-introduction. It will become so fluid that you will effortlessly answer interview questions and generally engage in conversation.

Sidebar: Overcoming Social Anxiety

- Consider coaching services offered by your school or career development office.
- Ask to be videotaped or practice with a career services professional.
- Record yourself on video or audio and then evaluate your performance. Ask trusted professionals at your school or within your circle to provide constructive feedback.
- Implement the suggested changes immediately.
- Seek opportunities to interact in the situations that make you uncomfortable and study your demeanor.
- Give yourself a break. Mistakes are part of the process.

Chapter 8
WRITE IT DOWN

Whenever I forget something I write it down. Stories abound concerning highly successful ideas that were conceived randomly and recorded for posterity onto a cocktail napkin. Writing helps people remember. And, reading someone's written work makes that person memorable.

Be memorable. Be a writer.

Unlike meeting people and finding creative ways to engage with the community, writing is the most flexible activity. It can be done at 4am on a Saturday, in between afternoon classes, or en route to a summer clerkship.

Someone once told me that writers write. They don't complicate the task at hand and they don't wait for the perfect moment. They write when they can and edit later. They also write about what they know or what they can find out from others. It is another form of engagement. It is the perfect opportunity to connect, both with a topic and with its constituency.

Law students have one great advantage over those who have already graduated. They are not practicing in a specific area of the law, in a single jurisdiction or in a particular sector (private, public, non-profit). As such, you can experiment with the type of writing and focus on a range of topics until you find one that speaks to you more deeply. Again, you have the opportunity to try a particular area on before committing, so take it.

Junior lawyers have a similar freedom, except they should allow their employers to review and comment on their written work. That said, practicing lawyers, even those so new they have not yet been admitted, often have more significant exposure to the experience of being a lawyer. That insight lends great richness to any written work on the topic.

The goal is twofold. First, it is to simply put finger to key and to become accustomed to the process of following up on ideas with outlines and rough drafts. Second, it is to publish.

There are many hopeful writers out there, particularly in law school. In fact, in a spring of 2007 survey of 2,500 lawyers for *The Lawyer* magazine, 40 per cent of lawyers in the United Kingdom indicated that they would have become either writers or journalists if they could have followed their dreams. The problem is that although they want to write (and most do in the form of motions, briefs and letters), they are not getting themselves published. When you get published, you want to get published again. You learn the value of writing for a wider audience and the tremendous benefits that effort produces.

It also serves to highlight how the law connects with the subject on which you are writing to your readers by applying legal issues to actual situations and personalities. It brings vibrancy to the field in a way that other activities cannot. It helps to celebrate the work you do, the people you meet and the ideas you have in a positive and notable way by allowing you to provide insight as a storyteller, rather than as a counselor. It is a vehicle for conveying both your persona and your expertise.

"It certainly doesn't hurt for resume-building either," says Eric Sinrod, a prolific writer and litigation partner in the San Francisco office of Duane Morris LLP. "It shows initiative and intellectual acumen," he adds. Employers evaluating two law students with equal credentials will often look for such qualities to make their decision.

In addition, those qualities reflect a different mindset and attitude. They serve to predict how an individual will approach the practice of law and the treatment of clients. They are a statement of character. They are qualities of a rainmaker. "Writing shows an ability to understand marketing," Sinrod notes.

Ultimately, if you write something well, you can very likely get it published because there are almost no barriers to entry. Alternatively, if you want to speak to a group, you have fewer assurances that you will receive an invitation to do so. For a law student or a junior lawyer, speaking is probably not a regular activity even if just from a scheduling perspective.

Consider, for example, a student that wants to write about new health care regulations. There are few organizations that will invite him or her to address their group (unless, of course, he or she has specific expertise and experience in the area). But, if that same student wants to write about the rules, he or she can meet with and interview experts, study the new changes and attend public presentations on the topic. He or she can then follow up those activities with a pitch to a local, regional or national publication about his or her efforts, expressing an interest in writing about it. If you don't believe it is possible, test yourself and see.

Remember: writers write.

Sidebar: Writing to Remember

- Writing connects your knowledge with the interest of your readers.
- It gives you a unique opportunity to connect with others in a meaningful way.
- There are no significant barriers to entry.

8.1 The Mechanics of Getting Published

Written work is very much like currency. One can use it to build a network, establish a reputation and gain general exposure. Most importantly for many, it has a tendency to remind the writer of the satisfying aspects of studying or practicing law. Law students, in particular, live in the unusual vacuum of theory and lose perspective on the most interesting aspects of their decision to acquire a legal education. They are afraid, tired or bored, depending on their class year. At each level though, as a group, they genuinely wish to be inspired.

That yearning for inspiration follows us into practice and loiters in our collective psyche. Writing responds to that need. It offers an opportunity to meet the people you find most interesting, to engage in meaningful discussions with the community and articulate your thoughts with clarity and insightfulness.

It gives others a reason to respond to your e-mail, return your voicemail and to remember your name. It also gives you a reason to send that e-mail, leave that voicemail and follow up. Everyone has an idea. Success is a result of executing more often than others on those ideas. "There is no substitute for just doing it," says Sinrod.

Sinrod has mastered the art of converting writing into a multi-million dollar book of business. In the late 1990s, he was representing the founder and head of Upside magazine in a legal matter. The staff was looking for a lawyer capable of writing a column on cyberlaw. They approached Sinrod and the rest is history. "My writing career happened accidentally," he says.

Sinrod notes that most attorneys don't write because the return is not immediate and tangible. It is also time-consuming for many. The weekly legal columnist for CNET News.com and Findlaw.com, who has also written for USAToday.com and *ComputerWorld,* among others, distinguished himself early by writing for his audience rather than his peers. "It is important to write in plain English, rather than to confuse people in either legalese or geektalk," he says. He also honed his craft so that he could write quickly and digest substantial amounts of information easily. He is now able to write a column in less than two hours. He recommends that hopeful authors just "start writing, start submitting and start building a portfolio."

You can write about the law, but if your idea is about scuba diving, modern art or heli-skiing, the benefits are the same. And, in the process, you become more interesting, which is exactly what Warren Jackson noted is critical in growing as a professional.

While it sounds daunting, the art of publishing requires nothing more than an understanding of how to select an appealing topic, where to seek publication, and when to pitch your idea. The details come with experience, but those three points are the most significant for beginning the process.

SIDEBAR: The Art of Getting Published
- Select a topic that has personal appeal and piques the curiosity of potential readers.
- Seek publication based on the audience and exposure.
- Pitch when your idea will be most relevant to the community.

8.1.1 TOPIC SELECTION

Despite late night feelings to the contrary, the law is fascinating. Television has popularized criminal and family law, and the media has focused extensively on financial issues. More obscure matters like space law, agriculture litigation and animal rights, among many others, offer significant prospects for a law student or junior lawyer to weigh in on an important subject. Those that can distance themselves from macro generalities and select a fine point that is particularly engaging can easily create the premise of a well-received article.

For those who cannot, the Internet is a great resource. Technology lawyers, for example, can find them on Gigalaw.com; consumer protection attorneys can visit FTC.gov. The variety is almost incalculable (at least for me). With no shortage of resources, the only hindrance to great commentary is one's imagination.

The most important consideration is the writer's level of interest in the subject. If it bores you, you will never finish the piece. If you are ambivalent, the piece will drain your time and energy before completion. For those reasons, select topics about which you are passionate or excited to learn more.

You do not need to be an expert or even familiar with the subject matter. You simply need to decide to pursue an area, even if your decision is general in nature. Many people get discouraged when trying to draft an outline without any familiarity. Don't be one of those people.

The secret is actually to ask someone. The beauty of writing is that it helps you organically engage with others in an honest attempt to learn more about their area of expertise. Students can ask professors, junior associates can ask partners and both groups can ask business leaders, politicians and others. Request an interview and ask an expert about your topic. After just a few minutes, you will understand the basic background and after fifteen or twenty, you will have a few ideas for the direction of your article. You will probably also have some powerful quotes, so take notes during your conversation.

Ask the first person with whom you speak for the name of another individual with familiarity in your area. To make it easy for you, set aside an hour or so for this process. Although your meeting should not take more than half an hour, I encourage you to try to meet with people in person. That human interaction is much richer and will have a greater impact on your day. If you have the opportunity to meet someone in his or her office, you will have a glimpse of what influences them and their work, which could provide additional connectivity between the two of you.

When someone helps you formulate an idea, he or she becomes linked to the article. You should keep him or her posted on your progress and the direction in which you have taken the original idea. You will also want to let that person know how your follow-up conversations went. That original interviewee is now the ideal source for fact-checking your work (assuming you feel comfortable asking for such guidance).

If possible, always try to recognize the expertise you receive from others by quoting them in the article when appropriate. You should also send a thank you note with the published piece. Depending on the evolution of your relationship from that first conversation, you may want to offer to buy breakfast or lunch as an expression of gratitude. In addition to being a kind gesture, it offers another chance to speak with and learn from this person.

This practice is especially effective for junior lawyers who ask colleagues, either more senior associates or partners, for guidance when writing an article. There is generally more opportunity to interact and the benefits will often be more immediate in that the discussion of the article is more likely to come up in conversation at the office.

You can help that discussion along if your article provides clarity on an issue with which people tend to become confused. Selecting a topic based on this idea can be very useful because lawyers frequently share articles they find helpful in their daily work. Law students will do the same and even blog about them.

Your work may not need to be focused on a typical legal issue. Instead, it could address practical advice, such as tips for successfully navigating a real estate closing or ideas for interviewing for a clerkship.

The key to topic selection is finding something that interests you and engages the reader. Since the best topics are the result of discussion with others, interaction is critical. If you speak with enough knowledgeable individuals, you are certain to identify a common area that needs some clarification. When you do, you have your idea.

For more detail, seek out additional resources and perspectives online. Ask your sources what the best websites may be for additional detail. Once there, those sites will inevitably lead to such information. You may also want to consider writing to experienced journalists who cover a particular beat. For instance, if you are working on a piece about electronic discovery, e-mail an editor at an e-discovery newsletter or a columnist at a technology website that might be able to guide you. While you will probably obtain important insight, you will further your sphere of influence. When you are ready to pitch your story, that editor or writer should be at the top of your list.

An experienced writer may not want to ask an editor for advice on developing a story idea, but a law student or practitioner beginning to develop a portfolio has more flexibility. The perception is different and, therefore, it is easier to seek assistance from non-traditional parties. Take advantage of this leniency to build as much credibility as possible.

Bear in mind that the value of writing is in the process and the experience. The level of scholarship is not always the critical factor, though quality is paramount. If you do not have the opportunity to write a law review article in school, you can still find publishing success that will help you plant seeds. In fact, with the time it would have taken to write one scholarly piece, you could probably complete three or four articles for more mainstream publications, such as a local newspaper or bar association magazine. "There is a huge demand for quality scholarship, particularly items focused locally," says Williams Kastner's Galanda.

By writing shorter more targeted pieces, you will also have the opportunity to meet exponentially more people and broaden your outlook in a much more diverse manner. The curious aspect of good topic selection is that it will often lead to ideas for follow-up articles.

SIDEBAR: Selecting Topics on Which to Write
- Identify an area in which you can provide clarity.
- Focus on practical issues for maximum appeal.
- Ask colleagues, friends and mentors for guidance on issues that interest them.
- Conduct preliminary research using the Internet and other available resources.

8.1.2 PUBLICATION PREFERENCE

Most people are under the misimpression that the largest publications are the most useful in terms of follow-up potential, as if publication in *The Wall Street Journal* will automatically lead to an opportunity to be a regular guest on CNN and a call from the general counsel of a Fortune 100 company requesting legal advice. Despite dreams to the contrary, neither of those is likely. In fact, for law students and junior lawyers, "the publication in which your work appears is not as important as the act of just getting published," says Fishman.

It is often a targeted newsletter that serves a few thousand people, all of whom have the ability to influence your future, which bears the most fruit. For a student or junior lawyer in particular, the benefit to getting published is in the act, rather than the result. And, if you did get published in *The Wall Street Journal* your first time out, where would you go from there?

Since this is meant to be a learning and growing process, select publications with editors that will appreciate your effort and give you constructive feedback. Your goal should be to work with people who will help you and build an assortment of strong writing on as wide a variety of topics as you choose. These venues will also allow you to experiment with substance and style, which is critical as you begin your career. Their staff may also serve as a resource for other publications.

After working with an editor, invite that person for lunch or a cup of coffee depending on his or her schedule. Most people will usually accept your invitation and you can treat the event less formally (though not casually). Get to know the editor and ask how he or she started in publishing. Be genuinely interested to learn more about that person and their aspirations. Express your appreciation for the publishing opportunity.

Closer to home, but no less potent are school newspapers. Law students and even recent alumni should not overlook publications that are either associated with the law school or, if available, the university at large. These are periodicals in which your work is almost certain to be accepted and usually have an impressive readership when including alumni and those in the community. Some school papers have circulations that are larger than mainstream newspapers. The *Columbia Daily Spectator,* for example, is one of largest dailies in New York City with a circulation of 10,000 serving a community of readers in excess of 60,000.

One of the most valuable ways to select a publication is to simply ask colleagues about the trade publications, newsletters and websites they read regularly. This will offer an opportunity for you to share your idea and interest in the particular subject. Your colleagues will most certainly appreciate your enthusiasm and share their ideas with you.

New lawyers should seek out the advice of the resident librarian or firm administrator. The person in this position responsible for subscriptions will typically have insider information on which newspapers and periodicals particular lawyers prefer. He or she will also know which employees at the firm are most interested in writing and getting published.

Law students have an even wider range of individuals from which to seek guidance. There is the law school librarian, but there are also career services professionals, professors and practitioners either on your advisory board or at your internship or other place of employment.

Consider who you would like to see this article, e.g., the chief litigation counsel for a medical equipment manufacturer, and find out what that person reads. You can ask colleagues or go directly to the source. You can also contact the sales department of the publication as its representatives will have that information readily available. It is also generally accessible online in the media kit magazines and newspapers use to solicit advertisers.

Don't forget fellow students and colleagues. With any luck, you are not the only one reading this book and so there may be others pursuing this particular option. Collaborate. Share ideas. Support one another with referrals and contacts. One of the unique aspects of writing is that there is absolutely no need for competition (a contrarian notion in law school, but one that exists in various pockets of reality).

Referring a fellow writer to a publication is helpful to the editors there because they are always in need of content and, of course, your colleague will appreciate your effort. Not only does writing give you the chance to do someone a favor by writing about them, it allows you to support their interest in the art as well. It is the rare activity in which everyone benefits equally and positively.

Both students and new entrants to the bar should look at the profiles of these professionals that they emulate and study the places in which their work has been published. If you see that a senior lawyer at a firm you respect has been published in a particular industry magazine, study that publication's website or obtain a copy and review its submission guidelines. Compile a list for future reference.

This exercise may even provide a justification to contact that lawyer. Sending an e-mail about an article that he or she published expressing an interest in pursuing a similar topic in the same magazine is as strong a reason as any to make a person's acquaintance. It will give you an easy opening line when contacting the editor, i.e., "Mr. Jones of Jones & Smith suggested that I contact you."

SIDEBAR: Publication Selection

- Think niche and local.
- Ask colleagues.
- Review profiles of prominent professionals and note where they have been published.
- Use the inquiry as an opportunity to meet new people.
- Refer friends and contacts to editors so that they can take advantage of similar opportunities.

In your search for the perfect home, do not forget online venues. Recall that the primary goal of getting published is to engage with others and demonstrate enthusiasm, not simply to see the item on the newsstand or even in print. In fact, Eric Sinrod has found great success writing for online-only venues like Law.com, CNET and Findlaw.

Looking online also serves to broaden your range and potentially your reach. Websites are seen by readers across the globe, which means that work published online becomes part of the fabric of the Internet. This is critically important because it makes you searchable. Most law students today are judged on their personal footprints that appear in the first few search engine results, but those who write, even online only, may be judged on their substantive work rather than their social faux pas.

Online publication can also lead to related online opportunities. Sinrod, for example, is a commentator for various Internet radio and television outlets.

Students with the added advantage of free access to research tools can study publications and find related opportunities more easily. Those no longer able to satisfy their research addictions with these fee-based tools can find tremendous resources on the Web. Conducting an advanced query using Google or Findlaw.com will lead to a variety of source material.

Below is a general list of potential publications for your research. Each has different requirements for publication, but the group will serve as a springboard to find many others. Analyze publications based on your audience and your goals. If you simply want to distribute your written work, any publication will suffice. In most instances, however, you will want to note the venue in which your work was published. As such, consider internally ranking a publication based on its readership, quality, distribution and respect among your peers.

Keep track of your research because it is possible that you will identify a publication that is not appropriate for the article on which you are currently working, but may be well-suited for your next project. Here is a fractional sample of what is available:

    Akron Legal News
    Alabama Law Weekly
    ABA Journal
    ACC Docket
    American Lawyer
    Asia Law
    Australian Lawyer
    California Bar Journal
    California Lawyer
    Central Ohio Source
    Chicago Daily Law Bulletin
    Connecticut Bar Journal
    Daily Journal
    Daily Record
    Divorce Magazine
    Family Law (UK)
    Finance & Commerce
    Florida Bar Journal
    GP Solo
    Illinois Bar Journal
    Indiana Lawyer
    Internet Lawyer
    Kentucky Bench & Bar
    Law & Order Magazine
    Law & Politics
    LawNow (Canada)
    Law Society Journal (Australia)

Law Talk (New Zealand)
Law Technology News (NZ & US)
The Lawyer (UK & New Zealand)
Lawyers Weekly
Legal Assistant Today
Legal Intelligencer
Legal Times
Los Angeles Lawyer
Massachusetts Lawyers Weekly
Metropolitan Corporate Counsel
Metropolitan News
Michigan Lawyers Weekly
Minnesota Law & Politics
Minnesota Lawyer
Missouri Lawyers Weekly
National Law Journal
New Jersey Law Journal
New Jersey Lawyer
New York State Bar Journal
New York Law Journal
North Carolina Lawyers Weekly
Oregon State Bar Bulletin
Rhode Island Lawyers Weekly
San Diego Source
San Francisco Attorney
South Carolina Lawyers Weekly
Texas Lawyer
The Recorder
Trials Digest
Virginia Lawyers Weekly
Wisconsin Lawyer Magazine

8.1.3 CONTACTING EDITORS

In your mind, editors should be no different than professors or partners. They should be respected and their schedules should be honored. "I treat my column like a client and my deadlines like a statute of limitations," notes Sinrod.

The first step is generally finding the appropriate person to contact. While there are often multiple individuals who edit content, there is usually only one who makes acceptance decisions. That is the person with whom you want to speak.

Start the process by looking either at the "Contact Us" page of the organization's website or the masthead of the printed version (usually found in a stand-alone section on the first few pages). While there is a temptation to contact the executive editor or the editor-in-chief, the managing editor is often the day-to-day decision maker on freelance submissions. There may even be a features or legal editor that is even more appropriate. Begin by contacting that individual and expressing an interest in writing for the publication.

Given that the entire writing process is about engagement. Consider using this as another opportunity to connect with colleagues, friends and acquaintances about their ideas. Mention that you are planning to pitch a series of magazines for a new article you are developing and ask whether they know the person who selects new writers. If it is a local publication, a prominent attorney, business executive or marketing professional may have the answer. In addition, now that he or she is involved, that person will have a vested interest in your success.

Once you have identified a contact, learn as much as you can about the individual and review the publication. Some editors also write and many have specific areas of interest. Like a job interview, the more you know, the more positively your inquiry will be received. For example, if an editor used to work for a technology magazine and is now with a legal-oriented newspaper, you can highlight some of your technology experience in your note and reference his or her prior work.

Bear in mind that the job of an editor is to find and incorporate material into the magazine that drives readership. Accordingly, your initial contact with the editor needs to be convincing. That said, you will likely only have a minute or two to convey your point, either in the time he or she will spend reading your e-mail or in your follow-up telephone call.

The deciding factors will be who you are, your topic and your time hook. For instance, on July 1, 2007, the Sunday edition of *The New York Times* published an op-ed written by former Vice President Al Gore about environmental activism because he was on the virtual eve of a climate change debate with the entire world through his Live Earth series of global concerts. Obviously he is someone of note, but his topic was compelling and his timing was ideal. Consider ways that you can raise an important issue on the eve of an event (e.g., an industry conference, a local anniversary, the enactment of a law, or an election) to which it is directly related.

SIDEBAR: Properly Contacting Editors

- Find the appropriate individual by visiting the "Contact Us" page of a publication's website or by reviewing its masthead.
- Direct your query to the Managing Editor over the Editor-in-Chief or Executive Editor.
- Study the background of the editor, if at all possible, in an effort to personalize your note.
- Treat any interaction with the same respect that you would incorporate into a job interview.

As always, use your status as a student or junior attorney to your advantage. Note your unique perspective as someone with just enough knowledge of the law to be dangerous, but not necessarily an expert. Highlight your ability to interest the publication's readers with the same level of enthusiasm with which you approach your own work. Sincerity is often an influential factor in contact selection decisions.

8.2 THE PITCH

One of the great benefits of pitching a story idea to a magazine or newspaper is that it requires the same skill that you will use throughout your career to achieve any goal for which acceptance by an unrelated third party is necessary. Becoming more comfortable with the process will have a wide-ranging impact as you develop.

To pitch successfully, be brief, be persuasive and be yourself. The idea is to induce your reader to follow-up and ask questions. It is not to write the story or provide a detailed outline. It is simply to give him or her enough information to decide to call or reply to your e-mail. Accordingly, it should not take very long. Do not over burden yourself with the pitch.

In addition, before sending anything, study the publication. Pay specific attention to the length of the articles, as well as their subject and tone. Try to determine where your idea might be best suited. If it is not likely to be accepted as a long feature story because those are primarily written in-house, perhaps your work would be acceptable for a special section in the front or back of the publication.

As part of this process, review the submission guidelines, which are usually posted on the publication's website. These are the rules that determine what appears in any given issue. They usually will provide general specifications on the length, subject, perspective (i.e., national, regional or local), style and, for many legal venues, whether footnotes are required. Be aware of these restrictions before reaching out because if you propose to write a 750-word article for a magazine that only accepts 1,500-word features, you weaken your candidacy.

Editors appreciate due diligence in the same way an interviewer or prospective client does. This advanced research may also help you determine the audience and focus your idea. Also, editors that recognize the efforts of a writer will more readily make suggestions concerning the subject or publication.

The preferred method of contact in the industry is e-mail. While you can call the editor directly, many are busy and would rather thoughtfully review and e-mail than ask questions over the phone. He or she will likely ask for a follow-up in writing anyway. The submission guidelines will often dictate the means of contact so verify your plan of action before implementation.

A common misconception about pitching an article is that prospective writers must complete the manuscript before reaching out to an editor. Actually, most publications do not want you to submit anything other than the three or four paragraphs described above. As a law student or practitioner, the last thing you want to spend your valuable time on is an article that will need to be completely changed or get rejected outright. Review the publication guidelines at the outset for this very reason.

This method will also allow you to formulate a number of different ideas without wasting time on a single item that may not have the greatest impact. Avoid spreading your suggestions too far and failing to track each one properly. You can easily do so by creating a schedule for follow-up using a spreadsheet or an online calendar. A calendar will also help you determine the lifespan of a particular article's relevancy and the duration of its time hook.

Despite the fact that you are not writing the entire piece, conducting extensive research in the form of interviews with possible sources and following an issue in the courts or the legislature is always beneficial. It helps you become familiar with the material so that you can speak informatively with interviewees, editors and colleagues.

SIDEBAR: Pitching Basics

- Do not send a finished article for review; send a short note indicating the idea, describing your background and highlighting the relevance of the story.
- Be brief, but persuasive.
- Study the publication and research the editor, if possible, before submitting your query.
- Make your initial contact via e-mail.

8.2.1 THE IDEA

Begin your initial query by describing what you would like to write, who you are and why you are ideally suited to author this piece. Be succinct, but potent. This note should be three, possibly four, paragraphs at most.

Your description of the idea should be concise, i.e., "I would like to write an article on the new SEC regulations on X and their impact on the market." If you have selected the publication properly, the people within that market are those who make up the readership. Thoughtfully consider that group of readers in your message. Add a sentence about what makes this issue so important to them. It is often the justification for the story and its impact on the audience that determines whether an editor will continue reading, rather than the subject itself. For this reason, include your strongest justification and indicate that there are others.

8.2.2 THE IDEAL WRITER

With respect to who you are, evaluate this question as well. I am not trying to get you into therapy, but spend some time on the description you plan to share with others. You are not just a law student or a lawyer. You have varied experience and enough credentials to get yourself published. You also have a certain expertise that the magazine needs and that the editorial or writing staff cannot likely provide.

If you are a student, indicate why a course of study enhances your qualifications. Similarly consider why prior summer or part-time work experience adds to your ability to provide a unique perspective. If applicable, note the individuals with whom you have spoken and the potential to quote them in your article.

Do not forget those factors that make up your entire profile. If you are from Brooklyn and there is some connection to the story, add that point. If you are a scuba diver, rock climber or novice botanist and there is some relationship to your article, add it. Background details often provide appeal and suggest that your perspective will be unique enough to attract readers. That attraction is a paramount concern so be certain to address it prominently.

SIDEBAR: Highlighting Expertise

- Consider why you are qualified to write on a particular topic.
- Apply your course of study, work experience and personal background to that evaluation.
- Avoid undervaluing your experience.

8.2.3 RELEVANCY IS KEY

Another critical factor to convey is what makes your topic relevant. If there is no time-hook for your story, selection is unlikely. Like Al Gore's op-ed, your story needs to be temporally connected to the community for which you are writing and speak to an issue about which its members are thinking at any given moment. This is the reason why we see so many holiday gift guides written in December and none written in the spring. That said, however, there are plenty of Mother's Day gift guides in mid-May and Father's Day articles in mid-June.

You need to identify why your proverbial gift guide would be relevant at a time that a reader would not expect. When the Federal Rules of Civil Procedure were amended to reflect changes in the management of electronic discovery in December of 2006, there were articles everywhere in November, December and January. Yet, there was not much coverage of the issue in April of 2007 because the issue was no longer timely. To relate it back to the public consciousness, you would need to link it to a current event or activity. Perhaps e-discovery was a critical factor in a recently decided case or is a budgetary concern for companies ending their fiscal year in June and evaluating purchases for the upcoming year.

Consider how you can make your story idea relevant, if that point is not obvious. Again, ask others why a particular issue may be of concern. And, when you properly conceptualize the piece based on someone else's suggestion and it is accepted for publication, let them know. A short note thanking a contact for his or her insight has long-term impact.

8.2.4 PRODUCING SAMPLES

The final piece of the pitching puzzle is the writing sample. Although you do not need to provide award-winning prose, you should include with your query an example of something you have written that looks similar to what you are proposing to write. Avoid term papers or briefs, but feel free to include clippings from school newspapers or student magazines. Work produced at an internship or other school-related outlet is also acceptable. If you produced something that does not have a byline, include a note that you are the author. Many publications will give you the benefit of the doubt.

If you do not have clips, there are always opportunities to obtain one by penning a book review. Be selective about what you cover, however, as some book reviews can be more interesting and valuable than others.

While you may have the freedom to select any book for review, I would suggest that you select a book written by someone in the area in which you want to practice or focus. Try to find an author who would actually appreciate your effort. For example, many attorneys write books that are never reviewed because they are not popular enough to garner the attention of the press. If you can find a book in your area written by an attorney or other professional with limited reviews, consider that particular item.

Feel free to contact the author and ask about ideal publications in which the review could appear. He or she may be able to give you a lead to the right contact. Follow up with a request to meet and pursue the various other points raised above about making friends instead of contacts.

You also have the option of submitting an editorial for a local or regional journal. Contrary to common practice, opinion page editors generally require a fully written article for consideration. You may be able to ask the editor if a certain idea would be likely to attract his or her interest, but such a response would be rare.

Take caution in that certain editorials can have a negative impact if you take a position that is contrary to the views held by many people with whom you work or would like to work. Focus on the positive aspect of an important issue and ask others for guidance. Your goal is only to have a published piece that you can use as a sample for future query letters.

SIDEBAR: Building a Portfolio
- Student publication clippings should be included as examples of your writing.
- While less desirable, unbylined works demonstrate your ability.
- Review a book written by an individual who would appreciate your effort.
- Consider editorials, but approach the subject with caution to avoid alienating certain readers.

8.2.5 CO-AUTHORSHIP

Co-authorship is an ideal way for law students and junior lawyers to secure placement of their work in a publication that otherwise would be impossible at their level. It provides you with exposure to new venues and an opportunity to collaborate with a respected practitioner or other professional. Writing together on a non-work-related project, but in an inventive specialized context, can lead to new and unexpected opportunities such as client referrals, new billable work and even friendships that transcend the law. It can also just be fun.

From the perspective of your co-writer, he or she gets an eager partner with whom to share the responsibility of pitching, writing and editing. Take on as much of the time-consuming tasks as possible and support all of your conclusions with well-founded research. Gingerly ensure that you are listed as a co-author on the byline so that you can actually use this article the next time you pitch.

STUDENTS TAKE NOTE: Law students working part-time or spending the summer with a firm should, if appropriate, follow an assignment with a suggestion to the assigning partner about the possibility of writing about a client or its matter (in general terms only). Some projects may even call for an interview with the client for a possible quote about an industry trend. At the close of the interview, ask about the magazines that the in-house legal team reads and circulates. Consider suggesting to the partner that he ask the client for other in-house contacts that may be appropriate for a short interview and quotation. This will help build relationships with prospects and offer new opportunities.

When you co-author with someone, your relationship becomes eternally memorialized in the published work. When someone searches for his or her name, that individual will find the article you wrote together. Similarly, when searches are made of the client representative or other interviewees, your name, the partner's name and the firm's name will all be connected. The Internet links the subject matter to the individuals and the organizations with which they are affiliated for posterity. And, you will very likely enjoy the experience as well.

SIDEBAR: Co-Authorship Works

- Consider the people with whom you would like to work and propose co-authoring an article.
- Make this partnership as easy as possible by narrowing down the topics, potential publications and other details.
- Propose ways to enhance your co-author's reputation and network.
- Ensure byline credit, if at all possible.

8.2.6 PITCHING ETIQUETTE

To limit confusion and tainting your reputation in the publishing industry, avoid pitching more than one periodical simultaneously. Make follow-up a priority, but contact your selected outlets based on your rank-ing system and fight the urge to pitch en masse. If more than one editor accepts your idea, you will have to disappoint someone. That disappoint-ment will, at a minimum, reflect your inexperience as a writer, and, at a maximum, ruin any possibility of writing for that person again.

Send your note by e-mail. It is quick, convenient and customary. Unless you have a relationship an editor or someone at the publication, avoid direct phone contact on your initial query. Also, give the editor a chance to respond. Wait three to five days before following up with another e-mail. If you have not heard back within ten days, call.

When you call, be prepared to give your pitch. Frequently, unsolic-ited e-mail will be lost in a spam filter so the editor may genuinely have missed your message. As such, when you call he or she may want to hear more. Be quick, but thorough. In addition, be flexible. The editor may indicate that the story might be more appropriate for a future issue. If so, thank him or her for the time and add a follow-up (with a reminder, of course) to your digital calendar.

Never give up. I hate to sound trite, but pitching requires endurance and self-confidence. Many people will reject your idea. Some will do it politely; others will have no regard for your feelings. Keep the names of the polite respondents and pitch them again in the future.

Frankly, keep the names of the rude people as well. Some may just have been in a bad mood when you wrote or spoke. Give people the benefit of the doubt and be self-confident. If your idea is a good one, it will have traction and you will find a believer. Incorporate suggestions to modify and resubmit to the individual providing the recommendation.

Think creatively about where you can see your work published. If you are writing in English, then it is possible for your article to be of interest to readers in any English-speaking country in the world. There may, however, be cultural distinctions in pitching overseas so prior re-view of the submission guidelines is critical.

Be professional in your correspondence and your demeanor. Avoid spelling errors, formatting problems and e-mail glitches. Proof your work before hitting the "send" button. Ask a friend or a colleague if your introduction and idea make sense to the reader. This will be helpful and offer another opportunity to connect.

Reach. If you would like to see your work in a newsstand magazine or newspaper, pitch the appropriate editors. You could get rejected the first (ten) time(s), but at some point, you may have a good idea in your area of expertise (even if that is being someone worried about billing your hours or navigating the interviewing process) that is perfectly timed. Similarly, if your work is so timely that it should be seen immediately, consider pitching television shows, radio and podcasts.

SIDEBAR: Proper Pitching
- Pitch your ideas to one publication at a time.
- Follow up by e-mail within one week.
- Be persistent, yet professional.

Chapter 9
Be Creative With Publishing

Every aspect of your written work has meaning. From the title to the tag line, you have an opportunity to convey a message and derive value from your work. These are not part of the relationship aspects of the writing process; they are about you and your creativity.

9.1 The Title

Occasionally, the editor will craft the title, but if you draft something appropriate and appealing, he or she will probably leave it alone. The key is to consider the message you are trying to send and the audience you are trying to reach with your article.

Jeff Zigler, a 2007 graduate of New York Law School, spent a semester studying at Southern Methodist University Dedman School of Law. He took a course related to food and drug law and wrote a paper about the dietary supplement industry, which he adapted for its February, 2007, publication in the *Food and Drug Law Journal*. The title: "A Free Market for Dietary Supplements: Issues Surrounding DSHEA's Exceptions to the Labeling Exemption for Third-Party Literature." "It was a great hot topic," Zigler says. As such, he wrote a descriptive title that would quickly gain the attention of practitioners in this area.

Galanda has honed this technique. The Seattle attorney has become a recognized expert in the area of Indian law with articles like "Know Your Local Laws When Insuring Indian Country"; "Getting Commercial in Indian Country"; and, "Leveraging Tribal Sovereign Economic Advantages to Attract Private Investment in Indian Country."

You can be witty, but don't make yourself look foolish. In addition, engage the prospective reader with a title that includes words related to their areas of interest. Galanda wants individuals doing business in "Indian Country" to read his work. Likewise, Zigler wants to ensure that those interested in "labeling" and "dietary supplements" are intrigued to explore further. Finally, bear in mind that articles written for trade publications may require pithy titles while journals and other research-oriented publications may allow for in-depth designations.

Regardless of the length you use, bear in mind that titles influence search engine results. In addition, using secondary titles in the body of your articles will have a similar impact, especially if designated as a heading when coded for publication online.

9.2 TAGLINE

While the first words are critical, the last are significant as well. Your tagline tells people who you are and what you do. While the publication may dictate how many words you have and what you cannot say, e.g., "He is looking for a job with a large law firm anywhere," you generally will have the freedom to write what you wish, so take advantage of the opportunity.

Obviously, identify yourself and your school or firm. Then add something unique about your course of study, summer experience or other endeavor. People read the tagline so give them something to remember. Then refer them somewhere for more information. Give them an e-mail address or a URL to your website. The link to your website will increase your search engine PageRank score. As a result, in the Google-everything era, this might be the most important step you take. The easier you are to find on the Internet, the easier it will be to stand out.

9.2.1. LEGAL ADVICE

We all learn in our Introduction to Ethics course, only lawyers can provide legal advice. Until you pass the bar and are admitted in your state, do not make the rookie mistake of inadvertently giving guidance you should not. There are a variety of ways of safeguarding against this so just be aware of the possibility.

First, avoid topics that require you to give people instructions. For instance, do not give people ten steps to do anything involving the law. The best articles for law students are those like Zigler's that provide report-like commentary on an important area. Creative students should, however, incorporate the perspective of practitioners and business leaders that would be affected by the new provisions, etc.

Second, add a disclaimer to all of your work that your article is for informational purposes only and should not be construed as legal advice. There are various ways of conveying this point. Feel free to reach out to professors, partners and others with more experience about appropriately crafting this point. Every question about your article, either substantive or procedural, can and should be an opportunity to engage with others. When asking questions, however, bunch them together. Instead of ten conversations or e-mails about separate issues, ask ten questions at once.

ASSOCIATES TAKE NOTE: Junior lawyers admitted to practice may have less concern than law students, but they should still incorporate a legal advice disclaimer. That last thing you need at a relatively new job is someone calling the firm at which you work claiming to have relied on the advice you gave in your article. Be clear and direct.

9.3 RETAINING THE COPYRIGHT

Most people do not think about the copyright to their written work, but if you don't make sure that you own it, the magazine, newspaper, newsletter or website for which you wrote it may prevent you from copying it. Most publications only want the right of first publication and the option of reprinting your bylined work in some type of anthology or archive. They do not necessarily want all of your rights forever, particularly those that do not pay their writers, so ask the editor about this issue if the contract he or she sends you indicates otherwise. Galanda adds "reserve all rights" in the footer of any article that he submits for publication.

One of the main purposes of writing is to share your work with others. You will also want them to share it with peers and friends. A copyright issue could stifle this process. While you could always direct recipients of your article announcement to the website that appears online, they may be disinclined to take that extra step.

That said, I would not jeopardize an opportunity to get published because of a copyright issue unless you have dramatic concerns. By at least providing the publisher with a non-exclusive license, it can reprint your work in related media and submit it for indexing in Lexis-Nexis. It should also be noted that if a link to your article on the publisher's website requires some type of registration or password, you will frustrate, rather than endear, your potential readers.

That may have a lingering effect when you send your next article. Set the tone early in your career and make people comfortable with what you are sending so that they recognize your work and have a sense of the branding. Always remember that you are building the foundation on which to create long-term connections. While students and new graduates may have some leeway because of their inexperience, that advantage will fade quickly if used unnecessarily.

9.4 Leveraging Published Work

Zigler knew that he could appear as a student with more than a passing interest in healthcare issues by distributing his article to law firm partners he had met while in law school (both in New York City and Dallas) and other medical professionals. Upon publication of his article, he wrote a cover letter summarizing his research on the new labeling law and providing a reminder on the basics of his background.

Students who use writing to enhance their profiles in school can then offer to write guest articles or, of course, co-author with law firm lawyers for industry newsletters. They can also pitch story ideas related to other general publications in their area of interest, citing the first article published. Some may even want to write to media professionals offering to serve as a commentator on the topic. Student radio and television shows, as well as podcast and online video programs, are appropriate venues to target at the outset.

For his first article called "Reservations of Right: An Introduction to Indian Law in Washington," which he published as a second year associate in December of 2001, Galanda adapted research that he had conducted in law school to form the nucleus of his piece. He offered similar articles to publications throughout the Pacific Northwest and volunteered to speak at different events on related topics. He is now chairman of the ABA Business Law Section's Committee on Gaming Law.

Stacey Gray creates opportunities by sending periodic newsletters to her network via e-mail. "It gives potential and current clients, colleagues and friends an update on the current legal issues and an idea about what you are doing in general. The newsletter allows them to feel like they are growing with you as an attorney and a business," she says. "One's newsletter should be both information and succinct, because the meaning of your communication will be lost if you provide too much information," she adds.

As a law student, these actions are all prep work, notes Tom Kane. "You can even do things aimed at the city or area where you hope to end up practicing law." You have the luxury of experimenting with the subject matter and prospective venues. Send a few newsletters and press releases to see what reaction you get. Note your mistakes and correct them in the future. Pay close attention to the suggestions that your mentor and others provide, and implement them immediately. As always, let them know you did so.

9.4.1 Starting Early

Another advantage of starting to write in law school is that by the time you get to a firm, it will be more difficult for supervisors to question the potential for distraction. Some people may not value your efforts to write as a junior associate, cautions Sinrod. They will wonder, "If you are going to spend all of your time writing, how do I know you are going to bill your hours?" he adds.

If you are hired with the expectation that you will continue the very writing that made you an attractive prospect, it is less likely someone will be skeptical of your motivation and commitment. You can write at your leisure in an effort to pursue issues that genuinely interest you, as Zigler did with food and drug labeling issues. In fact, soon after starting a permanent position, Zigler co-authored an article with a colleague.

It is always about gradations of dedication. You need to decide where you fall on the spectrum. Making that decision early in your career will significantly enhance your potential for success.

Sidebar: The Details of Getting Published

- Make your title pithy, catchy and alluring to prospective readers in your target market.
- Draft your tagline carefully so that it says enough about you for readers to follow-up and learn more. Include a means of contact, such as your e-mail address or website URL.
- To avoid the appearance of providing legal advice, include a legal advice disclaimer.
- Whenever possible, ensure retention of your copyrights by discussing the issue with your editor or noting the reservation of rights on documents that you submit. Avoid jeopardizing your publication opportunity over this issue unless you have significant concerns.

- Distribute your writing inside and beyond your personal network. Use it to enhance your profile by offering yourself as someone with knowledge of a particular area of interest.
- Starting to write as early in your law school tenure as possible will enhance your candidacy as a job prospect. It will also give employers an understanding of the activities that you will continue to pursue as you grow in your legal career.

9.5 Publishing It Yourself

The subject matter of your written work is less important than the fact that you make the effort to share it with others. Getting published is all about the conveyance of ideas, both your own and those with whom you speak (providing proper attribution, of course). It is also about building a bridge to your future. When you write, you stake a claim to a subject and add to the body of knowledge in that area. Once you do so, you can refer back to it and build on that principle for the future.

There are traditional methods of achieving this goal like pitching and less conventional techniques like self-publishing. Pitching has the advantage of securing placement in an established publication that readers typically know and trust. You can also target a specific group by pitching particular newspapers and magazines. And, distribution occurs naturally by virtue of that publication's channels in print and online. You simply have to persuade an editor to accept your work and then, of course, produce it.

You typically do not, however, have any influence over the layout and placement of your article. In addition, final editorial control is often in the hands of publication staff, which could mean last minute changes of a potentially substantive nature, including modifications to the title and the tagline, or deletion of certain quotes for space constraint reasons. You also need to share the publication with other writers, photographers, advertisers and others. The value is in writing the piece, connecting with others for its creation and distributing to your network as effectively as possible.

Self-publishing on the other hand offers a broad range of possibilities, including the opportunity to be the controlling force behind the production. The effort that distributing alone lacks initially in credibility and requires in terms of commitment, is rewarded in terms of breadth of your reach and potential for readership loyalty.

As the editor, publisher and creative content director of your own form of media, you have the chance to truly brand yourself. You can select content based on the individuals that you would like to highlight or work that you are enjoying at the moment. You can also encourage readers to subscribe to ensure that your e-mails are opened and read, sometimes with enthusiasm. Ultimately, you let your audience know who you are by the material you provide and the people with whom you associate. You become known as both an insightful commentator on important issues and a respected publisher.

Since the most successful lawyers can both craft the message and deliver it with power, you will demonstrate the skills necessary for success in the profession. Whether in a job interview or a client meeting, others will positively view your efforts. Interestingly, they will often do so without any sense as to your level of success. Again, it is the effort that carries the most weight.

9.5.1 Create Your Own Magazine

Arnold Peter of Raskin Peter Rubin & Simon LLP in Los Angeles was once the Vice President of Legal and Business Affairs for Universal Studios and served on the Board of Directors for the LA Chapter of the Association of Corporate Counsel. He felt, however, that his role as an in-house lawyer at an entertainment company was qualitatively different from that of most in-house practitioners. He was also inundated with newsletters, mailings and other material from law firms while serving in-house.

In an effort to connect with his peers and provide them with something of value, he established the Association of Media & Entertainment Counsel in late 2004. Along with the AMEC, he created a magazine for dealmakers and business affairs executives in the entertainment industry. His goal was to create a resource for the people responsible for production, distribution, sponsorship and advertising. He approached friends in the Global Entertainment and Media Practice Groups of PricewaterhouseCoopers and Korn Ferry International with his idea and together with his law firm they assembled Media & Entertainment Insight, a quarterly magazine about the business of the entertainment industry. Three years later, the magazine, which covers business, technology and legal issues, as well as industry profiles, has ballooned to a subscriber base of 30,000 and with advertising, it is now self-sustaining.

Peter's effort was remarkable for its direct simplicity as much as its novel approach to connecting with ideal client prospects. It captures all of the essential elements of how to use writing as the very foundation of business development. *M/E Insight* genuinely spotlights the industry on which he and his peers focus and highlights the excellent work of its legal counsel. It helps Peter build organic relationships and enhances his overall satisfaction. "I love what I do," he says.

STUDENTS TAKE NOTE: Law students shaking their heads thinking they cannot do the exact same thing may want to ask Rick Klau about starting his own law review in 1994 after his first year at the University of Richmond's T.C. Williams School of Law. Klau, the Strategic Partner Development Manager for Content Acquisition at Google, Inc. and former Vice President of Publisher Services at FeedBurner, was interested in the Internet and its implications for the law. "I was surprised to see that no one else was focused on those issues," he says. So he and his friends decided to start their own scholarly publication online to cover this area. "We started out thinking we'd do a traditional law journal, but quickly decided that publishing online would offer up tremendous advantages," he recalls.

By publishing on the Web, Klau and his team ensured that they would not just reach the traditional law review reader, but could connect with anyone interested in the profiled subjects. "I believe our readership was far broader than the typical law review reader," he notes.

With the advantage of faster publication and greater accessibility, the *Richmond Journal of Law & Technology* was born. At its inception, it focused broadly on technology because the Internet was new and intriguing. Today, it includes biotechnology, nanotechnology, general intellectual property matters and other topics.

"The Dean at the time, Joe Harbaugh, was extraordinarily supportive," Klau says. "Not only did his staff secure office space for us, they also provided some monetary support, and helped us in our presentation to the faculty to get academic credit for participating."

Credit aside, "when you start your own publication, you are the editor-in-chief and founder," says Ross Fishman. You have also built an impressive resume point for discussion and a specialty. The benefits also tend to outlast one's tenure as a student or even a practitioner.

Klau agrees. "Getting to be the first in the world is something you don't get many opportunities at, and it generated a tremendous amount of visibility for us as we were looking for jobs," he says. "Today, it remains an accomplishment I'm very proud of," he adds. In fact, Klau, who has spent over a decade with start-ups, and his staff, authored the *Blue Book* rule on citing online law journals.

Following in Klau's footsteps is possible for those willing to take the risk. Determine whether there is an area of law or the convergence of law and another topic that is being ignored. With the proliferation of blogging and other means of broadcasting, this effort is much easier than it was in the late 1990s. Still, it requires the same level of enthusiasm and motivation. "It was very difficult, but well worth it," he says.

Law students and junior lawyers with no budget can create a newsletter, e-zine or routine blog that covers an industry or trend. They can also do this under the auspices of their law school. Klau approached the dean of the law school and those who do the same are likely to be similarly welcomed. After all, it is in the administration's interest to see its students thrive and gain prominence, as Klau has done.

Even if you cannot develop your idea through the school, Fishman suggests just starting with a one- or two-page newsletter on a particular subject. "Make it electronic and call it a newsletter," he says. "No one needs to know that your circulation is eight people," he adds.

The act of creating the tangible item is the point. It is a unique activity that directly impacts the law, but the act of doing so is not necessarily related to the practice. Instead, it is a vehicle to learn about others, define yourself and guide others. It allows interaction in a way that fosters encouragement and understanding.

STUDENTS TAKE NOTE: For law students, these characteristics are ideal for making career decisions and evaluating the various paths the law provides. It helps one to make decisions about priorities and passions. "The law gives me a platform to do a variety of things," says Peter. "Practicing law is one of them."

Chapter 10
Blogging in Law School

STUDENTS TAKE NOTE: Blogging tends to be the white elephant in everyone's dorm or conference room these days. To blog or not to blog? That same question is on the minds of students and lawyers alike. For lawyers there are perceived pitfalls (mine is not to question their risk aversion, but only to recognize it). Law students, however, who do not blog should rethink their decision not to do so. If it is the result of either a dearth of ideas, concern over time or lack of motivation, then your choice is probably not well founded. "Blogs are like little doorways or windows to insight," says LexBlog's Kevin O'Keefe. "It is a living and breathing resume that allows you to network with students, professors, and lawyers," he adds.

Unlike any other tool available to students, a blog equalizes the playing field. It is the easiest way to get published because it is almost as simple as sending an e-mail. Its potential readership and distribution is broader than any publication to which a student or junior practitioner might have access. And, it provides a transparent way for one to demonstrate his or her knowledge and interest. "A blog is no different than who you are as a person," adds O'Keefe.

Those still skeptical should consider the efforts of Travis Hodgkins, a 3L at the University California's Hastings College of the Law. "When I started law school, I had never even heard of the blogosphere," he says. While few readers of this book are probably unfamiliar with the practice of online journaling, it is still relatively rare in school and throughout the profession generally. In fact, a quick search of Technorati or JD2B.com will reveal fewer law student blogs than one might think, though the list grows daily.

Bucking the trend, Hodgkins started writing about China for the Asia Business Law Blog during his first year after a few friends approached him because he was one of their few classmates who had been there or knew any Chinese. "Once I started writing for the blog and started receiving such positive feedback from readers, I was hooked," he says. He later founded the Transnational Law Blog. His work on the Asia Business Law Blog earned him widespread recognition and a position in Beijing the summer after his first year. His writing for the Transnational Law Blog garnered him a job in Shanghai for the summer after his second year.

For firms hiring law students, bloggers are a good bet. "You already know how they think and how they write," says Dan Harris, founder of Harris & Moure, PLLC in Seattle, Wash. and co-author of the award-winning China Law Blog. "To a certain extent you also know their personality so it reduces risk," he adds.

Harris is himself a prominent expert on Chinese legal issues and has seen his practice explode with the popularity of his postings. "Blog on what you know and love only," he cautions. "Don't blog to impress; blog to express."

For many, the art of writing online for a mass audience provides an opportunity to shape their voices and organically relate to others with similar interests. Whether you are a non-traditional law student pursuing a second career in an unusual location or a first-year associate establishing a presence in a new practice area, blogging offers a customizable way to get published on your own schedule using your unique situation and personality.

For Hodgkins, "it was a means for me to maintain contact with people and to continue learning international law," he says. One of those people was Dan Harris. In addition to serving as his blogging mentor, teaching him blogosphere etiquette and techniques for increasing readership, he was his employer in Shanghai.

Lawyers, academics, students (and even writers of books about writers of blogs) contact him on a regular basis. "Although networking was not my reason for blogging, it has been an obvious and unavoidable consequence of my work," he says. "My blog contacts have been so helpful that I never even bothered with the traditional on-campus interviewing process, which most of my classmates considered career suicide," he adds.

Even the law school's dean has been in touch. "Hastings has been very supportive of my blog," Hodgkins says. After Dean Nell Newton contacted him after reading a law professor's blog post that linked to the Transnational Law Blog, she invited him to co-sponsor a 2-day symposium about global warming (an event at which Al Gore and Nancy Pelosi could potentially speak). "In my eyes, it has elevated us to the status of a law journal," says Hodgkins.

All of the virtues aside, blogging is not as easy as it sounds. "Most lawyers are terrible bloggers," says Harris. "They are so afraid of offending people they neither impress anyone nor garner a readership." Start by studying those that manage the medium well. Ask questions. Seek advice. Participate.

Sidebar: Why Bother Blogging?

- At its core, a blog provides one with an opportunity to demonstrate his or her interest and enthusiasm for a particular subject. It also let's you showcase your talent and experience.
- Its scalability creates unforeseen opportunities by allowing you to broadcast your work worldwide via the Web.
- Online journals help connect their student authors with school officials, practitioners and others who can influence, mentor and inspire.

10.1 Getting Started

Google the term blogging and all of your questions will be answered. Unlike starting a print magazine or even an online e-zine, creating a blog is as easy as registering for a new e-mail account. There are free services, such as Blogger and Wordpress, and nominal paid services (starting at about $5/month), such as Typepad. They are all incredibly easy to use and offer similar tools. I spoke with students and practitioners that use both to equal success. Taking the Law.com blog network as an example, lawyers tend to use paid services that permit more extensive design for branding purposes, but otherwise, the value is in the content. In fact, a number of bloggers migrate from a free program to a paid platform when they start practicing or when their blog becomes popular enough to require additional features.

If you have comments to make on current events or a particular subject like the law or law school, blogging may be for you. Some bloggers weave in a discussion of how the topic on which they write impacts them personally using text, pictures and, of course, links to other blogs and web sites.

Amy Morganstern, 3L at the University of San Francisco Law School started her online journal two months into her first year. "I wanted to memorialize my journey to see how my focuses and writing style changed," she recalls. Above Supra on the Blogger platform (abovesupra. blogspot.com) receives about twenty hits per day from fellow law student bloggers and random search engine results. In addition to classmates, she has provided her URL to professors, attorneys and relatives. "It helps me to keep it clean and appropriate," she says.

Her posts range from informative to observational, but all contain a professional tone and an engaging style. On one day in the summer of 2007, she wrote about a the Ninth Circuit's decision in Perfect10 v. Visa, highlighting that "the majority (Judge Kozinski dissented) affirmed a motion to dismiss on claims of secondary copyright infringement." On another, she shared some thoughts on her summer internship at the Electronic Frontier Foundation. "We interns were advised that we can sit in on any meeting going on because they are 'open source,' although with a 'CC license,'" someone quipped. (CC is a reference to the Creative Commons license used by members of the online community to designate their preferred level of copyright protection.)

She has accepted an offer from Gunderson Dettmer Stough Villeneuve Franklin & Hachigian, LLP in Silicon Valley, which was impressed with her blogging. "When I interviewed there, I was told that one of the partners was pleased and intrigued to learn that I had a law blog," she says. During her second round of interviews, one of the attorneys asked her for the names of good legal tech blogs. "I think my blogging demonstrated that I was not only plugged into the tech scene, but that I was even participating in it."

That participation can have an impact downtown or over the border. Like Hodgkins, Morganstern has developed a network of contacts internationally through her blog and regularly corresponds with law students worldwide. "If I ever needed an attorney in Canada my blog network is the first place I would turn to," she says. In fact, she believes that blogs are a form of advertising in which a consumer seeks you out, rather than responds to an ad you place. It helps people find you.

Like many student bloggers, Morganstern incorporates a mix of enthusiasm for the law and a discussion of all things law school. "I have lots of quotes from my professors that I get a kick out of, excerpts from cases, things that only people in law school would be able to appreciate," she says. Writing about issues in a way that engages and informs gives prospective employers and clients a greater sense of your skill as a lawyer. Ultimately, people want to work with others they like, but who possess the level of skill they need. Blogging conveys both qualities. It is also a way to study the law in a more interactive fashion. "It is a place for me to mull over legal issues that I'm either writing about or to get feedback from others on what they think," she says.

Unlike many law student bloggers, Michael Rice spent ten years prior to law school as a software consultant for PricewaterhouseCoopers and for Intel Corporation's internal consulting group. He takes a practical approach to his legal education. "You can only learn so much in school," says the 2L from Seattle University School of Law who blogs at Coderights.com. A programmer at 14, he decided to become a lawyer after trying to build his own technology and realizing he liked the licensing aspects of the process best. "Contracts is endlessly fascinating to me," he notes.

He started blogging a year before he applied to school because he simply wanted something interesting to put on his personal statement. He was not sure of the value he could offer with Coderights, but wanted to create a way to remain in touch with his associates. "I am hoping that I can use Coderights as a tool for follow-up," he says. "The Internet lifts your voice a little bit about things in which your audience is interested," he adds.

If you are new to blogging and are trying to find your voice, there can be tremendous insecurity during the first three to twelve weeks, which writers consider the hardest. The antidote to this anxiety is diligence. While many bloggers begin their journey enthusiastically, the momentum is quickly lost when the burdens of consistency and creativity become too great. It must develop into a habit to get easier, but most bloggers give up before it does so, advises Rice.

It could also help you determine a potential area of practice. When Rice started blogging, for example, he maintained a strong interest in intellectual property matters. Once he was in school, however, he realized that IP was much more for scientists. He refocused on litigation or corporate transactions related to technology disputes.

Writing in this way also demonstrates vision and an understanding of what distinguishes the good from the great. It may be too early to tell whether nascent bloggers will require a special type of heavy-duty umbrella to control their rain, but by meaningfully connecting with others, demonstrating their skills and broadcasting their work in a virtually unlimited fashion, the odds are in their favor. "I don't think blogging is mainstream yet," says Morganstern. As such, there is tremendous opportunity for the taking.

SIDEBAR: Starting Up

- There is little to no financial cost to starting a blog.
- Posts can range from observational to substantive, but should have a professional tone.
- Writing regularly helps convey an understanding of the practical aspects of law school and helps the writer identify a preferred area of practice.
- The first three months tend to be the most difficult as it takes time to develop a routine.

10.2 WRITE ABOUT WHAT YOU KNOW (AND LIKE)

When Julie Elgar and the partners at Ford & Harrison LLP in Atlanta met with John Hellerman, they were looking for the right way to converse with their audience of employers and members of management to promote their successful employment litigation firm. Facing a website with relatively low traffic, the Ford & Harrison team partnered with a publishing company to support the technological issues and leverage its built-in network of readers. "We wanted to do something for legal in an entertaining and educational way," Elgar says.

The idea to use NBC's "The Office" as inspiration for a Ford & Harrison blog struck John Hellerman one night as he was watching the show, which focuses on the inappropriate behavior of the manager of a fictional paper supplier. Storylines often touch on a range of "hot" human resources issues (e.g., sexual innuendo, inter-office relationships, etc.) and once they end, Elgar posts an analysis estimating how much the politically incorrect behavior would cost real-life companies to defend in employment lawsuits. "That's What She Said" (http://www.hrhero-blogs.com/thatswhatshesaid) was born (the name, a double entendre for the manager's trademark punch line, and the fact that the blog would be authored by a female attorney).

For students and others contemplating a blog, "Identify the best way to communicate credibility and expertise through whatever channel," advises Hellerman. When you get it right, it works. Elgar's readership exceeds 12,000 on most Fridays after a new episode. (The show airs on Thursday nights.) The blog has since been mentioned in *Business Week*, *Wired*, *The New York Times*, *The London Times*, on CNN and elsewhere.

As a law student, Josh Claybourn had an experience similar to El-gar. When the second-year health care associate with Rudolph, Fine, Porter & Johnson in Evansville, IN was an Indiana University law student he created "In The Agora" with a friend. The eclectic blog for which he still writes with four other lawyers addresses currents events, cultural matters, and legal issues. In school, the local newspaper, which serves 200,000 people in the area, would often request permission to run excerpts of his blog postings in the opinion pages. "I developed name recognition in the community for that reason," he recalls. "Whenever there were stories about blogging, I was interviewed as the most well-known blogger in the area," he adds. Naturally, this impacted his candidacy at firms during his job search.

Like Elgar and Hodgkins, Claybourn chose to write about issues of interest to him personally. He knew that writing on topics that spoke to him would allow him to articulate a viewpoint that would attract readers over time. He started blogging under his eponymous URL in 2002 while studying as an undergraduate at Indiana University in Bloomington, IN. There were law professors from the school who also blogged, one of which was on the admissions committee. "I do think it helped with my application," recalls Claybourn. In addition, when he arrived at school he already had a blogging mentor.

After meeting classmates with similar viewpoints and interests, the group (consisting of a few non-law students as well) realized that if they pooled their talents they could increase readership. In October of 2004, soon after beginning his first year at Indiana Law, he helped launch "In the Agora" (http://www.intheagora.com), which now receives about 1,000 hits per day. When they post on a particularly sensitive topic, that number could rise thirty or forty fold.

The busy law student, who managed to graduate in the top quarter of his class, also created a blog for law school news and events that became daily reading for the entire school, serving as the de facto daily paper. When non-Christians claimed that a Christmas tree in the school lobby was offensive, Claybourn blogged about it, and it became national news covered by Fox and CNN, as well as on local television and radio stations. "I was very well known throughout all of Indianapolis because of the weblog," he says.

While Claybourn still would have secured a job without his writing, "there are big marketing advantages," he notes. Claybourn stands out among his peers as a thought leader. He is respected in his community for his thoughtful guidance and interest in sharing it with others. And, he did it by simply writing about what he knew, collaborating and providing knowledge on current events that was relevant to his audience (i.e., other law students and members of the local community).

10.3   Collaborate for Success

The benefits aside, "maintaining a blog is a serious time commitment," says Hodgkins. While the first blog to which he contributed suffered because of fighting between its founders, he notes that the best way to manage the posting schedule is by having multiple contributors. "Other people bring expertise to the blog and they add variety to the dialogue," he highlights. While he focuses on China, contributor and recent Hastings graduate Nema Milaninia is an authority on issues concerning Iran and the Middle East.

Lawyers have the same access. David Leffler writes for "Staring at Strangers" with his colleague, Jennifer Rose, who lives and works across the U.S. border in Morelia, Michoacán in Mexico.

Varied perspectives can enhance readership and increase popularity with the law school and throughout the broader community. It helps foster dialogue and brings people together in a way that generates long-standing relationships, which is the hallmark of co-authors.

Luke Gilman, a 2L in the evening program at the University of Houston Law Center blogging at LukeGilman.com for almost four years also participates in a group blog known as FirstMovers.org, created by Jim Chen, now Dean of Louisville Law School, when he was at the University of Minnesota Law School. Collaboration allows you to organically expand your network to include the contacts of your co-writers as well.

It also enhances the level of awareness that others have of your work. "I've met with a number of local attorneys who have become aware of me through the blog and more than once have e-mailed someone in the legal or blogging community only to discover that they already know who I am," he says.

Look for other bloggers at school or within your practice area with whom you might like to work. Hodgkins prominently places a notification on his site encouraging students with an interest in writing to contact him directly for more information. If you are unsure about starting your own blog, writing within a team of other more experienced bloggers may give you the practice you need to start your own venture, while offering many of the same benefits.

Timothy Ferriss, best-selling author of *The 4-Hour Workweek* (Crown, 2007) recommends inviting guest bloggers to create content. Conversely, guest post on other blogs as often as possible, and be creative. "This cross-pollination of audiences can double and triple your effective reach and beyond," he says. "Connect yourself to existing networks whenever possible," he adds.

The ultimate goal is to be a part of the conversation.

Sidebar: Joining Forces

- Blogging in concert with others can broaden an audience and enhance a blog's popularity.
- Collaboration allows one to leverage the networks of his or her co-authors.
- Writing initially within an existing team of bloggers may help new writers become acquainted with the blogging community.

10.4 Stay Committed

Persistence is often a major key to success in blogging. "The best advice I can give to anyone starting a blog is to never let it go dead," says Hodgkins. Those making a commitment to write need to maintain it throughout the year. While some post daily, weekly is also acceptable. "If you stop posting, then people stop reading, and starting up that momentum again is really hard to do," he adds.

Morganstern is in the top ten percent of her class, edited the Intellectual Property Law Bulletin and works as a research assistant for a professor, yet still manages to find the time to blog one or two posts per week. "It doesn't take that long because I have certain things stored up so by the time I sit down, I already know what I will cover." She estimates that a short post could take as few as ten minutes to write. That said, it used to take Rice an hour or two per day in the beginning. Now it takes him less than 3-4 hours each week to write 6-10 posts. Ferriss suggests writing posts in batches and repurposing material from multiple sources. "Interviews, books, and blogs all have different readers and listeners," he says. "Take the best from each and repurpose for the others."

Most bloggers, particularly students, slow their pace when their schedule becomes too busy to manage. "As long as you tell readers what is happening, it is acceptable to post less during exams," says Rice. He emphasizes that bloggers must build trust with their readers who want to see continuously updated content. Letting readers know why you are not posting will keep them coming back. "While time-consuming, I've found blogging to be well worth the effort and would recommend it to anyone," says Gilman.

He is taking the process one step further by planning a pilot podcast with a local attorney to serve as the guest host. He anticipates rotating hosts with ties in the legal community to discuss theoretical and practical aspects of particular subjects. "I'm hoping that this will not only raise my own profile, but that of the law center as well," he says.

SIDEBAR: Stay Committed

- To be successful, you must blog once or twice per week at a minimum.
- Consider the topics on which you will post in advance to save time drafting.
- Taking a hiatus for final exams or vacation is perfectly acceptable, but let your readers know the duration of your absence and encourage them to return on a particular date.

10.5 Be Cautious About Content

What you write in a blog is a direct reflection on who you are. "Students make the mistake of writing about their friends or unprofessional issues on their blogs, which can turn off the readers that they are trying to attract," adds Rice. "Your goal should be to stay on topic," he adds.

All bloggers, students and lawyers, must find a balance between information and opinion. That opinion can reflect a level of passion, but it should not cross the line. If it does, your writing could send the wrong message. "It can get you work just as easily as it can repel potential clients or employers," says Hodgkins. "If what you're putting out there is negative, then what you will reap is also going to be negative," he adds.

A blog is a means for readers to get to know you and your level of knowledge; ensure that it reflects both positively. Be professional in your demeanor and topic selection.

Morganstern cautions, "Employers will read your blog and it could impact your chances of getting a job." For that reason, many writers blog under an alias. There are obvious benefits and a sense of protection from retaliation for sharing controversial views. The advantages of self-identification, however, seem to far outweigh the perceived risks. "While many of my fellow students write anonymously, I opted to blog as myself," saysGilman.

In fact, other than publishing your views for personal reasons, there are few reasons to blog incognito. There would have been no job offer for Hodgkins, no recognition for Claybourn and no opportunities for Morganstern. (That said, of course, Jeremy Blachman created the highly successful "Anonymous Lawyer" blog as a Harvard law student, which he converted into a witty and entertaining satirical novel about the legal profession.)

"The blog has given me recognition in interesting ways," says Gilman. He often receives e-mails from the law center's faculty and administration when he mentions the school in a post, which in part led to his election as the 1L representative for the Evening Law Student Association. "I frequently become the voice of the section and I'm routinely asked to bring grievances or suggestions to the administration on behalf of other students," he notes. When the first-years wanted tenured professors, rather than adjuncts, to teach the introduction to research and writing course during the summer instead of the traditional school year, it was Gilman who spearheaded that effort. And, just to show that it is not all work and no play, when he blogged about Steve Levitt, the author of *Freakonomics* (William Morrow, 2006), the publisher sent him a galley of the book four months prior to its release. "I'm finding those I meet who find out about the blog are far more likely to take an interest and keep up with me through that medium," he adds.

SIDEBAR: Words of Caution

- Avoid excessively personal or negative commentary.
- There is generally no value in blogging anonymously (other than to creatively entertain).
- Blogs can serve as a platform to address and influence broader issues.

10.6 TRAFFIC TRICKS

There is an entire army of professionals dedicated to increasing the readership on a blog, but there are a few things that you can do to customize that plan and make your blog stand out. Certain techniques will also help to attract that audience of people you are trying to reach.

10.6.1 LINK & COMMENT

The easiest method with which to start is simply linking to other blogs and posting comments on their sites. "The blogosphere is about having an open dialogue with people and so you have to interact with their blogs," says Hodgkins.

Most blogging tools have a blogroll feature that allows you to create a list of other sites to which you want to refer your readers. While there is no limit to the number, choose your links according to your audience and the message you are trying to send.

When you do link to another site, it is perfectly acceptable to let that site's owner know and to ask for a reciprocal link in return. Commenting on their posts is also a popular way for you to gain recognition and persuade him or her to add you to his or her blogroll.

The mere act of linking to someone's site is reason enough to send an introductory e-mail. If he or she is a local practitioner, consider following up with an invitation for a cup of coffee. Bloggers are a relatively supportive community of writers. Just as Hodgkins found a mentor who ultimately offered him a dream summer job, you may develop a similar relationship.

Blogging, like all of the other ideas noted in this book, is yet another way to distinguish yourself, while enhancing your personal satisfaction within the law. It can be used to engage, inform and empower. You are already part of a community that maintains a commitment to legal understanding and when you blog, you become a part of a more elite group that seeks to increase the level of clarity in that population. As such, take every opportunity to meet those working on issues to which you can relate.

Sidebar: Creating Links

- Link to the blogs of others and ask for their link to your blog in return.
- Provide thoughtful comments on the blog posts in your area of interest.
- Use this practice as an opportunity to meet and engage with those writing locally.

10.6.2 Select Interesting Topics

Michael Rice is very methodical about the issues on which he writes. He regularly researches litigation that involves either a type of software a company involved in its sale or use. He generally looks for any new cases in federal court within a two-week period prior to his posting. While he occasionally obtains almost fifty results, many are inapplicable and he can sort through the hits to find the most interesting and geographically relevant (i.e., those in Seattle or in the western region of the country).

Law students have the advantage of free access to academic research, but practitioners can find cases on the USCourts.gov site related to their specific district or through LexisOne.com, a free case law research tool.

Writing about recent decisions is a good way for new bloggers to get acquainted with the medium while providing insightful commentary that may be useful to their readership. It allows you to serve as a resource to others, which will encourage them to return regularly.

While Josh Claybourn has found success blogging on an eclectic mix of topics, Rice and Amy Morganstern tend to focus on technology, while Travis Hodgkins is an authority on China. Establishing a niche provides a blogger with a reputation in a particular area and encourages commentary from others in that area. If your goal is to relate to people with similar interests and goals, then you may want to consider targeting your message.

Topic selection can significantly impact your readership and should be managed carefully. On days when Claybourn posts about something sensitive, his readership increases exponentially. Those tracking these numbers can use Google Analytics, which is a free tool that informs a blogger about his or her traffic. Rice, for example, has incorporated the code into his site and now knows that he receives about 200 hits per week from readers in Seattle and San Francisco. That level of detail keeps him motivated and also excited about reaching those individuals in his target market.

Sidebar: Topic Selection
- Write about what interests you and on topics that will attract your target audience.
- Find subjects that will create a conversation and prompt readers to leave comments.
- Use Google Analytics and similar tools to monitor size and location of traffic.

10.6.3 Use Names and Boldface Type

In the summer of 2007, Rice received the following comment to one of his postings:

Thank you for covering our defense of the [XYZ] litigation against [our client]. The case is ongoing. We have recently launched a blog for those accused of software piracy by [ABC]. I invite you take a look at it.

The lawyer found his posting because Rice puts the names of the lawyers and law firms working on the cases he cites directly into the posts. When they Google their names or otherwise search for information on the matter under discussion, they will find Coderights. "Often my posts will rank very highly on their name," he says.

To reach the right audience, identify those individuals by name or otherwise by the work they handle. If you are interested in working at a firm that counsels clients in a particular industry, mentioning the work of firms within that area is an ideal way to demonstrate your fervor a year or two before you ever need an interview. Similarly, if you are just starting to practice and want to develop a reputation for understanding the concerns of in-house counsel on a particular topic, citing rulings and regulatory changes for their benefit will help you and your firm stand out.

Since the most significant area of a blog post is often the title because many people will subscribe to an RSS feed that only indicates the title to a potential reader, consider putting the case name into the title. Rice uses this practice and received a phone call from a securities analyst who was interested in how he found the information on the case he discussed. Rice downloaded the order from the 9th Circuit and provided it to him within minutes.

In addition to the titles, incorporating boldface type into your posting is an effective way to underscore important text. The technical search engine spiders that crawl through your blog looking for key information recognize highlighted text more easily. "The people involved in these cases are very interested in any information that is available," says Rice. For that reason, make it easy for them to find key facts, names, citations and parties. If there is a unique term of art or government agency involved, consider using boldface type to emphasize those terms.

The irony is that cases tend to come to life for the writer when he or she adds commentary to them. There is a vibrancy about blogging in real time about issues that matter to the community that they impact most deeply. "You feel like your practice starts now," says Rice. He attributes that feeling to the sense of involvement that most people feel about the substance of their blogs. "You have more skin in the game," he adds.

Like short articles in periodicals, blogs tend to direct writers away from the perceived abstraction of law review articles. Just as clients and prospects prefer relevant concise guidance, so too do the readers of a blog. "They want to read the sexier stuff like their competitors just got sued," concludes Rice.

STUDENTS TAKE NOTE: Law students are in the best position to report on these issues because they are a source for facts with much more available time than even a first year associate (who has a billable hour requirement with which to tend). Students also find the real world much more interesting than events that occur in the state of "Model" (the crazy torts hypos notwithstanding). It gives the learning experience context.

"Three years from now, I won't sound like such a rookie," says Rice. "I have no idea if this will pay off professionally, but already the connections I've made have given me insight into the legal community that I otherwise would never have had," adds Gilman.

SIDEBAR: Traffic Jams

- Put case captions and law firm names in the title of your entry.
- Use boldface type to highlight key terms, names and facts.
- Give popular examples to put the issues into context for your readers.

Chapter 11
Broadcast Yourself

I f there is one activity in which law students and new practitioners fail to engage it is promotion. Not empty self-promotion, but publicizing their activities as they occur. Sometimes telling people about what you have done is more important than the act itself since without the notification, there would be no recognition of your work.

Law students have the advantage of being bold in a protected environment. As a student, you can try and fail with few repercussions. Most prospective employers will appreciate your effort. In fact, newly minted lawyers operate under the same cloak with other members of the bar and in-house law firm or agency support teams available to help make their ventures successful. In most instances, a student or junior attorney with a remotely good sense for letting others know about a successful event will find support among his or her peers and colleagues.

The key is to focus on the event, rather than the individual doing the promotion. Gabe Galanda is the master of this technique. His Northwest Indian Bar Association sends out periodic press releases about events that the bar association over which he once presided is doing. They include, for example, information about scholarships the group is awarding or Indian law issues it is addressing on behalf of the wider community. At the bottom, Galanda's name is discreetly listed as a contact. His method lets the reader know that he is associated with these efforts, but that the efforts themselves are the important aspects of the release. It is an honest and genuine way to let individuals within his network and beyond know what he is doing and why without ever saying a word about himself.

He started this practice as a very junior associate without a single client and continues it years later as an attorney with a lucrative practice that reaches into states across the country. Now, it is never seen as a promotional tool because he started the practice before he had anything but a true interest in the subject and issues to convey.

Setting the foundation for name recognition and business development before you will ever need it is critical. It eliminates all of the pressure associated with client generation and maintaining your livelihood. Every effort is an experiment and each allows for a much wider margin of error if started early and in earnest. And, you can seek out advice from your advisory board, practitioners and even potential competitors because you are innocuous in your apprentice status. There is a short window of opportunity, but the benefits could last for years and serve you well into your future.

Leveraging that period requires some calculated risk and a strong sense of self-confidence. Those who think they have nothing worthy of broadcasting are absolutely wrong. Moot court victories (even attempts), internship efforts, bar association memberships and student organization events can all be the subject of a public relations campaign of sorts.

Generally, the program requires you to draft a short paragraph or two about the activity and why it is important to the audience to which you are directing it. Then, start thinking about where to target the message. School newspapers and related media outlets (e.g., student-run radio and television stations) are good places to start. Leveraging the power of the blogosphere could also be very useful.

There should never be any pressure to succeed in these efforts. If they result in some positive coverage, you should certainly take note. That said, however, if they do not, you should remain unwavering in your objectives. As you learn more about how to position your work and the aspects of it that may be interesting to others, you will exponentially enhance your visibility before it is even necessary.

Again, if you ever have a question about whether something is worthy of transmission, ask your advisory board or your mentor. Or, use it as an opportunity to engage with someone with whom you would like to develop a relationship. It offers an ideal way to begin the conversation and puts you in the position of seeking insight from someone that you respect.

11.1 Press Conferences

When Ken Thompson and his partners sued Con Edison in connection with the steam pipe explosion in midtown Manhattan, there were ten news crews waiting to hear the announcement at their press conference. "They help to advance the ball and tell the story of clients," says the famed litigator who has never lost a trial.

Law students could engage in the same type of activity for clinical work, regardless of the type of cases. Whether you are dealing with administrative issues related to social security disability payments or the defense of a Guantánamo Bay detainee, you could use a press conference to announce major filings or events.

You will probably only get the school paper, a few bloggers and perhaps someone from the Dean's office, but it would be fun. If you happen to be working on an issue of local importance, such as a zoning variance or microenterprise venture in your community, local reporters may attend as well. Regardless of the attendees, it will also offer you the opportunity to rehearse so that when you, like Thompson, are involved in multi-million dollar litigation on behalf of your own client, you will know how to handle the press. Most importantly, it will start generating name recognition for you and notoriety for the good work of the clinic in which you are involved, particularly if it is not one of the more high profile areas of law.

The same applies to student bar association, volunteer and internship activities. Those who artfully conduct these types of events focus on these issues and the parties involved rather than their own profile. They become part of the background, but are inextricably linked to the story as its narrator.

Blogger Travis Hodgkins may have the opportunity to co-sponsor with his law school an event starring Al Gore and Nancy Pelosi. That is an event worthy of a press conference. The conference could focus on the good work of the school, the speakers and the other writers affiliated with his blog, but Hodgkins will certainly be connected to the event and media inquiries in a very influential way.

It will also provide another outlet for Hodgkins to leverage the permanence of information on the Internet by having his name and that of the blog he created linked to coverage of an event addressing important concerns and featuring two of the most noteworthy political figures of his generation.

And, sometimes, if these activities serve no other purpose, they make for a great story when interviewing for a job, meeting someone for the first time or speaking with a client prospect. Dr. Tara Weiss, a professor of English at Kingsborough Community College/CUNY in Brooklyn, New York often remarks, "It is the journey, not the destination." For law students and young lawyers searching for ways to distinguish themselves, this mantra is perfectly applicable.

Students should start the process by speaking with the clinic's professor, faculty advisor for his or her student organization or an internship supervisor. Ask for guidance on participating in or initiating a press conference practice when warranted. Volunteer to handle all of the details and explain that the focus will be on the activity and not your role in its success.

New associates can often make the same effort by addressing this idea with an immediate partner or practice group head, who can then raise it with a marketing director.

The idea may fail and if it does, you become known as the person who tried to hold a press conference, which is nothing like being the summer associate that embarrassed himself at the managing partner's barbeque. If it succeeds, which is more likely, then you become known as a creative thinker who celebrates the efforts of others.

The choice is yours.

SIDEBAR: Press Conferences

- Hold the conference to celebrate the event or issue in which you are involved, rather than yourself in any way.
- Invite student and local media, especially if the issue has implications for the broader community.
- Even a failed attempt will enhance your reputation as a creative thinker and individual working toward the success of those whose work you were trying to recognize.

11.2 STUDY THE MEDIA

The importance of a press conference highlights how the media will be the primary way through which you communicate to your audience as you grow and your target demographic evolves. To prepare, John Hellerman suggests watching 60 Minutes, Dateline, Squawk Box and similar shows to learn how to identify and evaluate the messages being delivered. "Look for quotes from lawyers and other legal experts and try to determine why the reporter picked that statement," he advises.

To help you think like a journalist, Rex Bossert, editor-in-chief for *The National Law Journal*, suggests that you look at the kinds of stories in the publication on which you are focused and use them as a guide for pitching others. "Try to see the trend beyond the individual case, which will help the reporter or editor see a bigger, more potentially newsworthy picture," he notes.

Reporters in the legal press are often former attorneys who pursued their passion for journalism. Ashby Jones, for instance, was an associate with Perkins Coie in Seattle and a prominent writer for various ALM Media, Inc. publications before becoming Legal Editor for *The Wall Street Journal Online* in 2005.

They can empathize with law students and may be more likely than those in the mainstream to take the time to speak with you and share their ideas about publicity in the industry. Try to meet a legal reporter for breakfast, lunch or coffee. Be flexible as some publications are very intense first thing in the morning, while others have a more fluid workday. That said, breakfast is probably an ideal way to get to know one another. It takes place before the day becomes too hectic, there is no trouble getting a table (unlike at every coffee house in the country) and it makes for a relatively affordable get-together. Some legal journalists have never been contacted by a law student or junior lawyer. Be the first.

Ask the person with whom you are meeting (whether a reporter or an editor) what stories interest him or her. Also, determine when. The one key component of media attention is the timing factor, which is often overlooked. If you can develop an understanding of when the press needs to know about your story, you can plan with laser precision.

When you can provide great legal work to your firm and others with whom you are collaborating, as well as an intuitive understanding of organic publicity, you will create tremendous good will. You will also develop the skills necessary to promote your own work when the time comes. "It is important to get your legs," says Hellerman.

In fact, Hellerman has been hired by senior associates to handle personal publicity in their quest for partnership, one in particular who was passed over once before. They hired him to send the message that they are aggressive and entrepreneurial; their respective firms promoted them both.

Law students and junior lawyers can start engaging with the media by participating in projects that are newsworthy. For example, 3L Frank Seminerio's role as school representative to the ABA while Penn State is moving campuses has given him unique exposure to the local coverage. And, when reporters contacted Josh Claybourn about his blog in law school, he learned first-hand how to respond. The junior associate now has an incredible pool of experience from which to draw for his benefit and that of his law firm.

You should also consider attending events that will have associated media coverage. "Getting on a reporter's Rolodex is great, but you get there by doing other things," instructs DirecTV's Jackson. He notes that some individuals use golf, while others use wine tasting events. If UC Hastings and Travis Hodgkins ultimately persuade Vice President Gore or House Speaker Pelosi to chair the school's symposium, there is sure to be media attendance, and students who assist in the logistics of the program may serve as resources to them.

Hubbard One's Nancy Manzo encourages law students and junior lawyers to stay in touch with journalists in their preferred area of practice. "If you start making yourself available to reporters, they will quote you, and you will therefore become known as the expert on that topic," she notes. Manzo also recommends serving as helpful resources to journalists. If an opportunity arises, put him or her in touch with a partner at your firm or a law professor with whom you are familiar. Even if you or your firm is not involved in the legal issue at hand, you can still offer background (with your firm's approval, of course). This offers a remarkable opportunity to those fresh out of school and trying to prove themselves at a firm.

Students Take Note: Studying mainstream publications to learn how to think about the press and getting to know the periodicals that cover the universe in which you operate will help. The *ABA Student Lawyer* and the *National Jurist* are two magazines that focus on law school and legal career issues. There are also websites, such as JD2B.com, that focus on student concerns. Read these publications and study their messaging. Pitch ideas to the editor and learn what distinguishes and attractive story from one that is rejected outright.

In addition, ask the lawyers with whom you work, either in a clinic, at an internship, over the summer or as you begin practicing, what periodicals they read and value. Start by getting to know those in particular, since your direct colleagues have respect for them and would appreciate understanding how to leverage their value when an opportunity presents itself.

The one advantage that law students and fresh recruits have over their more seasoned peers is that they can contact junior level counterparts in the media and learn at their pace. It is much easier for a twenty-something lawyer to contact a twenty-something production assistant or junior copyeditor at a major newspaper than for a senior partner to do so. As you grow, so too will your contact. He or she will probably move between various news outlets over the course of his or her career just as you may move firms. When he or she leaves an existing position, ask for a referral to someone at the old company so that you can begin a new relationship at that location. Over time, you will have contacts at every organization where your contact spent time, with whom you will be able to mature and learn.

Finally, be the media. Start a podcast as Gilman has done. Blog, of course. Develop your own public access cable television show. Conduct interviews on a video blog. Be a resource for information.

When Claybourn started his blog about events at Indiana University Law School, he was simply trying to share information. It was only when that information covered a controversial Christmas tree in the school's public meeting area that his blog entries gained national attention. If you begin with what you know and simply start telling people about it with the intent of conveying useful knowledge, you will develop an appreciation for the role of the media. Shortly, that appreciation will become insight.

SIDEBAR: Learning About the Media

- Watch news programs to understand quote and story selection.
- Contact former attorneys that are now journalists.
- Start learning about publications focused on law school and the issues facing new entrants to the profession.
- Attend law school or local events that will attract the media.
- Get to know your junior counterparts in the media, including journalism students and members of the student press.

- Be the media. Blog, podcast, vidcast, or start your own public access cable television show.

11.3 ASSEMBLE PANELS

In January of 2006, Stacey Gray hosted "A Call to Action: Diversity Includes Retaining Minority and Women Owned Law Firms" in Midtown Manhattan. Her panelists included: Joaquin Carbonell, General Counsel of Cingular; Jason Brown, in-house counsel at Pepsi Americas; and Andrea Clark. 100 people attended the event and it earned a mention in *The New York Times*. A fan of group discussions on hot topics, she encourages students and new attorneys to make the effort to assemble similar events. "Panels on the right topic give you the opportunity to demonstrate your intelligence and leadership abilities," she says. They can also have a significant professional impact. "I have made back the investment I put in four- or five-fold," she adds.

Students have the opportunity to approach anyone and ask them to share their experience and perspective. Successful professionals as a class generally appreciate and enjoy these requests. Junior practitioners who are not far from school often enjoy this same "halo effect" in contacting others. It is often as simple as sending an e-mail or making a phone call.

Consider starting with someone who has mentored you or served on your personal advisory board. For these people, it will be an acknowledgement of their efforts in guiding you. They will have many reasons to participate and few not to. Your job will be to make it as effortless as possible, and minimize their time constrains.

STUDENTS TAKE NOTE: In the preliminary stages, approach a faculty member with whom you are in close contact and the dean, if possible. Once the school is involved, you will have access to its public relations team and facilities. The situation is almost identical to that which Christy Burke employs in her creative alumni programs. And, with a university endorsement, the potential for publicity and to demonstrate their own expertise as panelists, many individuals immediately accept the invitation. In fact, your initiative alone will garner respect. "You get the kudos before you earn it, but one must dedicate herself to hosting a successful event because your reputation will precede you for years to come," notes Gray about the value of panel discussions.

Select topics that will engage fellow students and professionals alike. Galanda galvanized the bar recently by campaigning to include questions about Indian legal issues on the Washington state bar exam. His work captivated the entire legal community at all levels. Your panel should do the same. Although most of you probably think of panels as grand symposia on macro legal issues like the state of the Supreme Court or universal health care, a panel can be about anything, even law school or life as a junior associate.

While Gray included a cross-section of in-house personalities for her "Call to Action" event, she generally selects her panels based on the topic and goal of the event. While you can broaden the perspective that you offer since you should be interacting with lawyers and non-lawyers alike, clearly identify your purpose for contacting local businesspeople, artists, politicians and others that may energize your discussion. Your favorite professor can also serve as a great resource given the vast connections that he or she likely has in the legal and business community. Ken Thompson's professor at NYU, who became the Undersecretary of the Treasury for Enforcement and now serves as the Executive Director for Interpol, was certainly a great resource for him.

STUDENTS TAKE NOTE: A diverse group can assist with marketing and expanding the potential audience. If your program is positioned properly, it may have appeal to law school alumni and graduates of the university at large. With that in mind, be sure to leverage the power of the Internet by persuading the school to offer your panel as a streaming video program or, at the very least, video on demand that can be accessed on the school's website and distributed via e-mail to its alumni (presumably tens of thousands of professionals). Take the initiative to write the copy for the e-mail if that will make it easier for the alumni department. You have the opportunity to contact each of the panelists and act as the liaison between the law school's administration and the prospective contributors.

You will become synonymous with the event and linked with its success. Assuming that you remain in touch with these individuals, including those who may be unable to join the discussion, you could build longstanding relationships with them. The benefit of panel discussions is that members suggest other members for you to contact. One lawyer may have a client who would make a perfect addition to your group or a colleague who represents the other side and can provide the contrary perspective. For you, it is just about having the opportunity to work with and learn from these individuals. It demonstrates your sincere interest in the law.

You can also serve in some way as the moderator of the program or by introducing the panelists. Remember that the focus of the program is on the subject matter and the participants, but as the creator of the event, you can certainly reflect publicly on why the issues are so important and express your appreciation for the time and effort of those involved. Gray notes as the architect of a unique speaking series, people begin to associate you with that type of event. They view you as someone interesting with a passion for a particular subject and a concern for sharing that information with others.

Engaging in these activities during the preliminary or early stages of your career allows you to solidify a reputation before you need one. Many of your law school classmates and colleagues will become the in-house lawyers and corporate executives that may someday hire you. If their perception of you as an individual is strong early on, they are more likely to remain in touch and associate you with a positive memory many years later.

It is not all fun and games, however, says Gray. "There are so many bumps in the road where you are tested throughout your career," she notes. "One must balance being aggressive about one's career with patience and diligence. Building and maintaining professional relationships are challenging because people are busy and have differing objectives at times." Occasionally, someone will not respond and scheduling conflicts arise at the last minute that can alter other plans. The logistics involved in these activities alone can be time-consuming and divert energy from studying and working, but must be balanced with current responsibilities. For larger events, consider partnering with another law student or junior associate that may be able to share the burden. This will also give you the chance to incorporate another individual into your circle and share whatever credit is appropriate.

Collaborating with a practitioner, particularly a peer who is only a year or two more senior will give him or her an opportunity to showcase his or her own experience alongside yours, but from a completely different perspective. If you could find an alumnus of your law school to join you, the administration would likely embrace the idea of a current student/junior lawyer alumni partnership and enhance its promotion with that aspect in mind.

That connection would enable you to gain name recognition with the associate's law firm partners and colleagues. Assembling a panel, unlike other efforts, allows you to speak directly with respected members of the professional community, develop a strong and positive reputation, and dramatically enhance your network. Although there can be a significant time commitment, it is generally manageable and can be shared.

SIDEBAR: Panel Presentations

- Take advantage of your "halo effect" as a student or junior lawyer when contacting members of the community to request participation in panel discussions.
- Start by engaging with a member of your network.
- Seek out endorsement of your law school or law firm.
- Select topics that captivate a broad audience, including alumni across the globe.
- Leverage the power of the Internet to reach remote alumni through Web casting and streaming video.
- Be cautious with your time to avoid compromising academic and billing commitments.
- Consider collaborating with a recent graduate.

Chapter 12
Raising Your Profile

A round 1990, Ross Fishman became the Chairman of the American Bar Association's Marketing Legal Services Committee. He was also its only member. Soon after joining, he doubled the membership when his supervisor came on board. The national committee with over 300 members recently celebrated its tenth anniversary. "I needed to build my marketing resume like law students and younger lawyers need to," recalls Fishman.

Similarly, when Galanda wanted to establish himself as an expert in Indian law in 2003, he ran for president of an organization that merely consisted of twenty-one names on an e-mail list. Today, the organization counts hundreds of lawyers and law students nationwide among its membership. It holds regular meetings and has distributed almost $100,000 in scholarships.

STUDENTS TAKE NOTE: By raising their respective groups to prominence, Fishman and Galanda positioned themselves as recognized experts in the process. Those interested in following their lead need to simply consider how to present their expertise through a leadership position. "ABA committees are great because there are so many of them," says Fishman. But, there are many opportunities, he adds.

Consider your area of interest and creatively merge that with a leadership position of some type. Start by reviewing the number of student organizations at your school. At George Washington University Law School (my alma mater), there are almost fifty student organizations listed on the school's website. They include common items like the Student Bar Association and Phi Alpha Delta, purportedly the world's largest legal fraternity with chapters in nearly every law school, and unique offerings such as the National Security Law Association, which likely takes advantage of being in the nation's capital by inviting local speakers to address its members.

While Texas Tech University School of Law lists a student bar association and Phi Alpha Delta as well, its students have started the Mineral Law Interest Group to address issues surrounding legal concerns related to water, oil and gas.

Like panel discussions and other events in which students take the initiative, schools are generally receptive to ideas about new organizations that meet a need. It adds to the collection of offerings for prospects, but it also provides an opportunity to invite esteemed guests into the law school in a niche area and develop your professional network. If you are a law student and want to start, for example, the Radio Frequency Identification (an increasingly popular technology issue) Association, start by simply e-mailing the dean of student affairs. Once established, you will be the leader of your own association.

Imagine how much more credibility you will have when contacting someone by introducing yourself as the President of the XYZ Association at your law school. Nobody needs to know that the group has no members. They will come.

Those students who create niche groups like the mineral law students at Texas Tech demonstrate by their actions a much more profound interest in a particular practice area than their peers. During a job interview, they can not only discuss the subject matter, but the passion for the issues that drove them to start an entire organization. They may also know experts in the field with whom an interviewer is familiar.

Like every unusual activity mentioned in this book, this relatively minimal effort will create longstanding relationships that have the potential to follow a student beyond law school and into practice. They also serve as opportunities to acknowledge the efforts of business and community leaders through a forum that you create under the auspices of your association. And, of course, it can be a lot of fun.

ASSOCIATES TAKE NOTE: Junior lawyers have even more opportunity. While they cannot create student organizations, they can assemble alumni groups and have access to local and national bar associations. When the leaders of the Mineral Law Interest Group graduate, they can establish the Mineral Law Interest Group Alumni Association through the school and follow all of the steps outlined by Christy Burke to harness the power and influence of the niche community to which they speak. Or, they can review the special sections available through the State Bar of Texas, for example, and determine how to fill a need with a section that does not yet exist.

This leadership can also extend beyond the law to community groups, political activities and charitable organizations. The point is to be the leader, rather than to lead a particular class of professionals. As you learn the skills necessary to plan events, delegate responsibilities, and promote the entity for which you are responsible, you become more adept at doing those things for yourself. You become empowered by empowering others. And, since you are the boss, you get to do it on your own schedule.

Like being the editor-in-chief of your own magazine and the moderator of an esteemed panel, leading a team (even one that starts off with nobody to lead) raises your profile by spotlighting the work of others. In the early stages of self-promotion, you can simply be a vehicle through which to spotlight the good work of your peers and mentors. As the leader of the group, you will ultimately be seen as the source for all information related to that sector. When local papers needed a quote from the ABA on marketing, they sought out Fishman.

McKesson's Jill Desallines recommends that you become the go-to person for something, anything. She suggests that you help people seeking information in your area of expertise. "You might do that for 10 people and when an issue comes up in your area, who will they think of?"

Be the leader that people seek by being yourself.

SIDEBAR: Assuming a Leadership Position

- Find something of interest to you and create an organization that you can lead in connection with that subject.
- Positions of management enhance the perception that you are an expert.
- The membership count of your group is almost irrelevant.
- Look to bar and community associations for opportunities as well.
- Leaders develop relationships that have the potential to follow a student beyond law school and into practice.
- Direct others on your schedule, if at all possible, and by being yourself.

12.1 USE TECHNOLOGY TO ENHANCE YOUR VISIBILITY

In 2006, Beverly Hills criminal defense attorney Allison Margolin spent a few thousand dollars to produce a video promoting her relatively new law practice representing petty drug offenders. The three-minute montage film was a hit and earned the 30-year-old Harvard Law grad tremendous name recognition. Over a year later, YouTube viewers have played her video almost 30,000 times.

Despite Margolin's success, Fishman cautions students and junior practitioners that "audio and video are hard to do well and easier to do embarrassingly badly." He notes that rainmakers do not build the perception of expertise by doing something that shows them in an amateurish light. Neither should you. "Anything you do has to be great," Fishman adds.

There is also the expense. Margolin spent about $5,000 to make her film. Most law students have a nightmarish Mt. Everest of debt waiting for them upon graduation. They have no interest in accumulating even more. And, while new lawyers finally have some income, most of it is spent on those loan payments, Starbucks and, presumably, any new product that Apple launches. (iPhone, anyone?) For those reasons, Fishman suggests that you audio- and video-tape every speech or presentation that you make. You can then upload the video to a You-Tube-like service and embed it into your website. In fact, you can get two pieces of promotional material for the price of one by transcribing your speech, editing it and posting it as an article to your website or even seeking publication somewhere. It is completely free and offers you the opportunity to be seen far outside of your immediate circle of contacts. It also provides a professional and polished image of you that will make a much deeper impression than simply words in an e-mail message.

Technology in many respects has leveled the playing field for practitioners nationwide.

Those who embrace technology become part of the fabric of the Internet and are more readily accessible by individuals searching for people who fit specific hiring criteria. Today, when someone meets you at an event and they go back to their office and type in your name, the information that a search engine returns could mean the difference between a follow-up call and instant rejection. The watershed event is people realizing that they need to be Googleable, remarks Nancy Roberts Linder. A blog, for example, is completely indexed by Google.

Students active in bar associations who connect their names with particular events that are advertised on the Web become forever linked with that topic and that organization. Generally, law students tend to do what everyone else does. In fact, the system almost mandates conformity. That said, however, technology allows them to be different. You just need to know the tricks that allow you to showcase your total knowledge instead of just your status as another law student from yet another law school.

Like online video, social networking has tremendous potential for those interested in standing out. While the scene began as the playground of the under-30 crowd, 53-year-old Richard Salzman of Hollywood, Florida started a solo practice in 2006 and created a MySpace page. His profile offering per diem services in Miami has already generated clients. "It doesn't cost anything and I am an optimist."

For next-generation members of the bar, now is the time to be thinking about how to leverage the tools you are using or recently used in school. Although more senior lawyers have successfully navigated through this maze, those of you with years of experience customizing social networking tools, such as MySpace and Facebook will only need to modify your approach slightly (and remove those spring break photos) to begin harnessing their power. Many professionals prefer Linked In and more corporate-styled programs. Whatever your choice, use it first for the benefit of those you are trying to meet.

When, for example, a headhunter contacts you with a job prospect for which you are wholly unqualified, share that information with someone in your network that may be a suitable fit. Whether he or she gets the job is irrelevant. That person will remember your thoughtfulness. Pay special attention to those with whom you work and develop an understanding of what they are hoping to accomplish. Find ways to leverage your network toward that end.

Stevan Lieberman, a partner with Greenberg & Lieberman in Washington, D.C. finds those ways in the virtual world as well as the real one. The intellectual property attorney joined the self-described "3-D virtual world" to enhance his presence in the offline world. By interacting with the other almost nine million "residents" of the website opened to the public in 2003, he reaches a new demographic. "I can market while sitting on my couch," he says. Lieberman notes that while Second Life (SecondLife.com) is not the only virtual reality environment, it has more adults who participate and can be more easily modified.

Second Life makes people feel as if they have physically met one another, Lieberman says. In addition, its interactive capabilities help users, particularly lawyers, to clarify difficult concepts. "IP law is extraordinarily complicated and a 3-D image helps people to reach out and touch items so that they can understand my explanations."

For those who are confused, "Second Life is not another world; it is an extension of real life," Lieberman explains. While it is free to enter and browse, there is a nominal cost to buying land and establishing an office or other presence. He has so far spent $200 and retained $10,000 in new business. While he recommends that law students and new lawyers interact in a virtual reality environment, he warns against inadvertently providing legal advice.

You may also be cautious in the avatar (umm, digital representation of yourself) that you use. While Lieberman has used figures ranging from someone with a flaming head to one with wings, law students and junior attorneys may want to present a less outrageous and certainly non-offensive persona. Although creativity is of value, you are winning points for just participating in this novel experiment.

Despite the uncertainties surrounding your use of technology, the benefits generally outweigh the risks. Before embarking on this path, seek guidance from more seasoned professors and practitioners. In fact, ask them to join you and consider learning together. Senior lawyers are intrigued by these new potential sources of revenue, despite their outward risk aversion toward them. If you take the initiative to help them learn, they will be more likely to teach you in return. Help someone on your advisory board film a presentation and post in online. Or, transcribe an audio speech into a potential article. By doing so, you are helping, but also developing a strong understanding of how to leverage these tools for your own use later when it matters most.

Finally, associates should clear these activities with their law firms. Mention it as an experiment to the partners. It could become a renowned success like Elgar's blog and garner prestigious headlines, or not. Again, if your firm has reservations, help someone else outside incorporate technology into their practice. When your firm is ready, you will have all of the necessary skills to be a groundbreaker in that area. It is the perfect way to plant seeds for your future.

SIDEBAR: Technology Trendsetting

- Use online audio and video wisely. Start by videotaping speeches and presentations.
- Convert transcriptions of audio and video programs into website copy and potential articles for publication.
- Social networking and virtual reality sites can enhance your profile.
- Be conservative in your initial appearance online and avoid sharing any information that could be misconstrued as legal advice.
- When in doubt ask someone you trust for guidance.

12.2 CREATE YOUR OWN CABLE TELEVISION SHOW

Video resume pioneer David Schnurman had television in his blood. In 1983, his parents, Alan J. Schnurman and Judy Stein, launched Lawline, a half-hour interview-style television show focusing on current legal issues. Since the show airs throughout the New York metropolitan area, it has access to millions of viewers. Twenty-five years later, the show is still popular among the legal cognoscenti and David is making his mark on "the family business."

As a New York Law School 2L, he started a public access cable television show on the Manhattan Neighborhood Network in New York City. The public access station offers residents of the borough a completely free opportunity to broadcast programming throughout Gotham on its various channels. Interested in entrepreneurship, Schnurman decided to start interviewing small business owners and sharing those interviews with his audience. That company, TrueNYC, has produced over 100 episodes since its inception and Schnurman has vastly expanded his network.

Interviews with the founder of Marquis Jet or the creator of The Baby Einstein Company enhance his own profile, while promoting and celebrating the achievements of those he meets. And, it is all broadcast directly into the homes of millions of New Yorkers, and streams over the Internet at TrueNYC.com, absolutely free.

Alan Schnurman, the host and creator of Lawline, realized decades ago that "cable was a terrific vehicle to be in people's homes that I did not know." He notes that there are about 60,000 lawyers in Manhattan and to differentiate oneself from the other 59,999, one needs to have a specialty, vast experience or a unique distinction. "You could be the best lawyer, a spectacular litigator and can know your subject up and down the street, but unless you get the work you will be out of business," he says.

After two and half decades on the air as the host and founder of what is purportedly the longest running cable show focusing on law in the United States, the senior Schnurman has had tremendous business success. Like most marketing and advertising, "it takes a long time," he advises. It took Schnurman years to develop a consistent source of inquiries because most people do not focus on something without substantial repetition. Schnurman's golden rule is that "all advertising works, but some attempts are more cost efficient than others." Lawline, which is filmed in Brooklyn, started on public access, but migrated to leased access shortly after it began taping. The program is on television every day somewhere in the New York Metropolitan area.

The recognition gained by serving as a talk show host on issues related to the legal community is significant. "Most people think about the monetary benefit, but if you're well known, colleagues and even judges treat you differently," Alan Schnurman says. On his first show, Schnurman, a prominent personal injury lawyer and real estate investor, hosted two well-known real estate lawyers for a live call-in program. The trio discussed the difference between co-ops and condominiums.

Ask yourself what subject you would like to discuss and whom you could invite on the show to address that issue. In 1983, cable was the only means to broadcast on a large scale. Today, however, you can do it with online video and a small video camera (or even a Web cam). The only obstacle stopping most people is simply a lack of motivation. Everything else is there for the taking.

Even if you only broadcast the interview to your personal network, your interview subject may share it with his or her contacts. The mere act of video or even audio taping your subject will alter the perception of who you are and the potential that you have. David Schnurman generally walks into the offices of people he meets today the same way he did as a law student a few years ago, carrying a handheld consumer grade digital camera, a microphone, a light and a seamless backdrop.

Those individuals who become affiliated with a public access network can even borrow the type of equipment that David Schnurman uses to film TrueNYC, as well as reserve space similar to what his father uses to film Lawline. Most stations will require registration and a multi-day training certification before permitting full usage. That said, there are worse ways to spend your free time.

Of his experience, Alan Schnurman says, "I love it, and getting to know my guests, who are people that I would never ever have had an opportunity to meet if we didn't have the show." Law students and junior lawyers have the same potential to meet individuals with whom they otherwise would have no opportunity to speak. Again, the newest members of the profession ironically have the lowest barriers to develop relationships and find rewards for their creativity. A public access show can provide a forum for you to build these connections an hour per week or less frequently depending on your schedule. Alan Schnurman actually films multiple segments of Lawline in a single day. In two and a half decades, he has amassed an archive of over 600 hours of interviews. Multiply that by two or three guests and the undeniable benefit to his reputation, spirit and business development potential is exponential. The same could be true for you.

SIDEBAR: Producing Your Own TV Show
- Research the public access stations in your area. (The list below is a good place to start. SOURCE: http://en.wikipedia.org/wiki/Public_access_television#Public_access_organizations.)
- Create a concept for a television show. Interview programs are generally the easiest to produce.
- Select prospective guests that you are interested in meeting and who will intrigue your audience.
- Be prepared to invest time training on new equipment and meeting certain familiarity standards set forth by the television stations.

PUBLIC ACCESS TELEVISION STATIONS ACROSS THE UNITED STATES

ARKANSAS

–Community Access Television CAT TV, Channel 18, Fayetteville

CALIFORNIA

–CommunityTV.org Community Television of Santa Cruz County

–Community Media Center Community Media Center of Santa Rosa

–Access Healdsburg Community TV for Northern Sonoma County

–Mountain Community Television MCTV 15, Weed

COLORADO

–Denver Open Media

WASHINGTON, D.C.

–Public Access Corporation of the District of Columbia, Channels 10, 11, 95 and 96

FLORIDA

–Tampa Bay Community Network Channels 19 and 20 on BHN Cable and Channels 30 and 36 on Verizon Cable, Tampa

GEORGIA

–Community TV-25 Cable Channel 25, Atlanta

IDAHO

–Treasure Valley Community Television Cable Channels 11 & 98, Boise

–Pocatello Vision 12 Cable Channels 11 & 12, Pocatello

ILLINOIS

–Comcast Public Access Serving the suburbs of Chicago

–CAN TV Chicago Access Network Television

INDIANA

–Sigecom cable offers Public access television, and educational content on Channel 9, Evansville & Newburg

–Insight cable offers Public access television and government meetings on Channel 7, Evansville

MASSACHUSETTS
–M8 and WMCTMarlborough Cable Trust and M8
–Amherst Community Television, Amherst
–Falmouth Community Television, Falmouth
–Fall River Community Television, Fall River
–Lynn Community Access + Media Television
–Medford Community Access Television
–Quincy Access Television, Quincy
–Randolph Community Television, RCTV, Randolph
–WCCA TV 13 Public Access Media Center in Worcester
–Cambridge Community Television, public access media
  center on channels 9, 10 and 22 in Cambridge
–Plymouth Area Community Television, public access
  media center in Plymouth
–East Bridgewater Community Television, Public Access
  Channels 9 & 98 in East Bridgewater
–Lowell Telecommunications Corporation, Community
  Media and Technology Center serving Lowell
–Brookline Access Television (BATV), informing the public
  with local and access-center programming.
–Burlington Cable Access Television.

MAINE
–Boothbay Region Community Television, starring you!
–Harpswell Community TV W14CLCable channel 14,
  LPTV UHF channel 14

MICHIGAN
–Clarkston Public Access Center CPAC CTV10
–GRTV Public Access Grand Rapids, MI

MINNESOTA
–CTV15 Public access for the inner north suburbs of the
  Twin Cities
–North Metro 15 Public access for the outer north suburbs
–Moorhead Community Access Television Public access
  for the city of Moorhead

MISSOURI
–KDHX TV 21 & 22 Public access in St. Louis

NEW HAMSHIRE
–Cheshire TV on Channel 8 in Keene, Marlborough, and
 Swanzey
–Valley Vision quality community access in the Mount
 Washington Valley

NORTH CAROLINA
–The People's Channel, public-access station in Chapel Hill

NORTH DAKOTA
–Community Access Television, cable Channel 12 in Bismarck

NEW YORK
–Bronxnet, a group of public-access channels in the Bronx,
 located at Lehman College
–BCAT, Brooklyn Community Access Television, several
 public-access channels in Brooklyn
–QPTV, Queens Public Television, Public access Channels
 34,35,56 & 57 in Queens
–MNN, Manhattan Neighborhood Network, Public access
 Channels TW 34 / RCN 83 TW 56 / RCN 84 TW 57 /
 RCN 85 TW 67 / RCN 86

OHIO
–Hudson Cable Television Channels 9 & 25 in Hudson

OREGON
–Portland Community Media Channels 11, 21, 23, & 30
 in Portland
–Rogue Valley Television Channel 9, Ashland

PENNSYLVANIA
–Peters Township Community Television Channels 7,
 17, 19 in Peters Township, McMurray

RHODE ISLAND
–PATV18 COX Communications Public Access, Public
 access Channel 18 in greater Rhode Island

TEXAS
–Austin PACT Channels 10,11, & 16 in Austin

VIRGINIA
–Arlington Independent Media, Channel 69 Arlington County

–Blacksburg Community Access, WTOB Channel 2 serving Blacksburg

–Charlottesville Public Access Television Channels 10, 13 and 14, serving Charlottesville and surrounding counties

–Fairfax Public Access Channels 10, 30 and 37 in Fairfax County

–Falls Church Community Television, PEG station serving Falls Church, a suburb of Washington DC

WASHINGTON

–TCTV Olympia Thurston Community Television

–SCAN Seattle Community Access Network

–PSA Kent Puget Sound Access

WISCONSIN

–Chippewa Valley Community Television(CTV) Public access Channels 11 & 12 in Eau Claire

–MATA Community Media (MCM) Public access Channels 14 & 96 in Milwaukee

–WSCS TV-8 Public access Channel 8 in Sheboygan

WEST VIRGINIA

–SCTV Summersville Community Television

Chapter 13
Be Your Own Public Relations Firm

Lawyers mistrust the media, but often because they cannot figure out how to coexist within its universe. Clients, however, generally understand what that relationship requires and how to benefit. In fact, they embrace it as regularly as possible. For that reason, law students and junior lawyers should evaluate how clients and potential clients are handling their public relations. Develop a fluency in the language of PR and ask those in your inner circle for a referral to an expert in the area. Ask him or her to coffee and listen. Ask questions, but mostly just listen.

Learn how to identify a message that will be attractive to reporters and others. Consider ways to customize that message to make it timely and beneficial to your various endeavors. Law students can use this knowledge in clinic activities, student organizations and as they achieve certain milestones. New associates have the same capability, but should review their activities with a partner or other supervisor at their firms.

Start by compiling a list of local media outlets, including print, radio, television and those online. Be sure to include satellite radio, podcasts and public access cable television. Don't underestimate the value of student media. A story picked up by a student wire service could end up in newspapers all over the country (and possibly the world).

Once you know where to send the information, begin drafting press releases for distribution. This should include your hometown periodicals as well, even if they are not local, says Tom Kane of the LegalMarketing-Blog.com. Make it more formal and consider sending a note even when you are appointed to law review or moot court. "Think of things that are newsworthy even if they don't shake the earth," Kane says. A community likes to celebrate its residents and will embrace the news of your success, regardless of how you value the particular accomplishment cited.

Don't forget about career announcements either, says Nancy Manzo. While most newcomers to the practice only provide them to their limited group of friends and family, Kane recommends that you also send them to your high school and college newspapers, as well as alumni magazines. For students, this announcement could even be about graduation itself.

Practitioners should coordinate professional announcements with their firms. "Get your name in the professional journals," says John

Herbert, who is in-house counsel at Pfizer. "I make a mental note and read the profiles of these people," he says. "If they do something that seems to be out of the ordinary in terms of what the multitude of people do in a given practice area, I may have occasion to call on them."

The exercise in PR is the most important part of this process. You may have little success at first, but eventually someone will pick up your story. When they do, you will develop name recognition and deeper insight into how to navigate the route in the future. This knowledge also becomes part of the value that you bring to a job or case.

Most importantly, however, is what it will mean to you five years from that point. Most first and second year associates are not thinking about these aspects of relationship management, but the earlier you start, the more potential for success you create.

Always remember that your goal should not be instant gratification. Rather, it should be one with a long-term view. If business development is indeed like investing, then your study of public relations should be from the "buy and hold" school of thought. "If you keep doing it over the years, you vastly expand your network," notes Kane.

That network expansion may come in the form of journalists with whom you develop relationships or colleagues with whom you work, but it could also start with an e-mail that someone sends you after reading about a recent clinic victory that was profiled in the local community paper.

While there are professionals who spend their careers focusing on PR, you should not be devoting that level of time to this effort. Instead, you should recognize when opportunities for press arise and seize them. It should not be a burdensome part of your work, but a satisfying enhancement to it.

Once you figure out the basics, share them with others. Those others could be classmates, as well as professors, practicing lawyers and members of your advisory board. Your effort to unlock the great self-promotion mysteries will win praise from those to whom you convey them. Ultimately, it will be a means to an end, notably greater fulfillment and an ability to help others.

Helping others stand out and network themselves can be very effective over time, says Darren Ofsink, a securities lawyer who graduated from Brooklyn Law School in 1994 and started the 21-lawyer Guzov

Ofsink with a partner in 2001. Law students interested in this effort should support supervising attorneys in understanding the nuances of what clients do and the types of business in which they may be interested. Students can spend the time that more senior lawyers do not have reading information on the Web and in niche periodicals that is relevant to a client's business, rather than simply the client itself.

When interviewing someone for an article or speaking with him or her about a panel appearance, find out how he or she defines professional success, and keep his or her definition in mind when moving forward. If an opportunity presents itself, consider ways to promote that victory.

Ofsink notes that this level of consideration often helps to network clients with each other. "People typically do not realize that two members of their network may benefit from meeting," he says. Make the introduction yourself or at least suggest that those senior to you make the connection. "You build up credit with people like that," Ofsink highlights. You also develop a reputation as someone who thinks of others and wants to help foster their success.

For law students and junior lawyers, the mere attempt to comprehend someone's industry or business model helps to demonstrate a level of sophistication, which enhances your ability to speak to clients with confidence, remarks Ofsink. "If you can show people that you can speak authoritatively and give practical answers, they will come back to you," he says. "In fact, they will not only come back to you, they will recommend you to other people," he adds.

Ultimately, learning how to support colleagues, friends and professional contacts trains one to recognize a business development opportunity. "There are plenty of clients that need things and sources to get those needs filled," Ofsink notes. Law students often do not see this aspect of relationship-building, but those that do are far ahead of their classmates. Learning this process requires an effort to leave the office, whether that space is in a clinic or a firm with a nameplate outside the door featuring the letters e-s-q after your name. "You have to stay in front of people," says Ofsink.

Staying in front of your audience is key because publicity alone is not enough, says Nixon Peabody's Cathy Fleming. She had the extraordinary good fortune to work on cases repeatedly profiled on the front page of both *The New York Times* and *The Wall Street Journal* in the mid-1990s. It did not, however, produce a single new matter. "Having great press in a case doesn't necessarily lead to business," she says. The press did, however, add credibility to her resume.

There is a combination of having people see you and making an effort to remind them of who you are that bears the most fruit. A high profile alone will not reward you for your efforts as effectively as an increased level of interactivity. The more people get to know you and your reputation, the more they want to see you succeed, says DirecTV's Jackson. "You do feel like if I get the opportunity to give them some work I am going to try to make it happen," he says.

In your junior years, you also have the chance to generate a reputation for yourself that will remain everlasting. Most practitioners are not thinking about the ideas with which their network associates them. Eventually, one becomes a tax lawyer and that is how the perception is forged. Those still in school or just starting out can engage potential members of their network with issues other than the law. Perhaps you have made a documentary film or are also a renowned athlete (on the side). Everyone has a dream that is typically different from what they are doing professionally, even if they love their jobs. If you can somehow tap into that side, you will become more than a contact.

Dan Rootenberg is a prominent physical therapist in midtown Manhattan and founder of the Spear Center for Physical Therapy. He is also a baseball player. In fact, he was the first person selected to participate in the Israel Baseball League, which brought baseball to the Middle East during the summer of 2007. Rootenberg took a sabbatical from his practice to play for the Netanya Tigers from June through August. "All of my clients know about my baseball career," he says. As a physical therapist, it almost makes sense to be a professional athlete. "They are extremely supportive and interested," he adds.

Sometimes it is just a conversation starter. "It is an ice breaker that simultaneously seems to add credibility to what I do," notes Rootenberg. It also helps with the self-broadcast by demonstrating your expertise and enthusiasm for something that complements your work "Having a unique talent, experience, hobby or cause may help give you the perception of more depth of personality or character," he adds.

Be yourself, but do so while letting people know who you are. "A lot of it is personality and a willingness to get out there," says William A. Chamberlain, the Assistant Dean for Career Strategy & Advancement at Northwestern University School of Law. Law students and junior practitioners have more flexibility in their early years so they should take calculated risks to extend themselves outside their sphere of comfort.

"Don't forget about your passions when you become a lawyer or develop in the profession," says Marci Alboher, a lawyer herself and the author of *One Person, Multiple Careers* (Business Plus, 2007), as well as a columnist and blogger for *The New York Times*. "Try to make room for them or try to integrate them into your practice and interact with people," she adds.

Alboher equates the value of a side passion with a fluency in a foreign language or a unique cultural understanding. "Your multi-dimensionality can help you get ahead," she notes.

Contrary to the popular myth that law students and junior associates cannot spend any time on anything but studying or work, Alboher highlights that your outside pursuits help you hold on to your identity and maintain your sanity. "It often keeps you balanced when you are moving between different things," she adds.

By way of example, she is an experienced traveler. As a junior associate, she would assist her supervising partner when planning his family vacations. She was able to fuel her passion, but also had the opportunity to become much better acquainted with her boss and his family. "It gave us something to talk about," she recalls. It also enriched their relationship and her professional experience. In fact, she advises "if you have something to which you are really committed and in which you have confidence, it equalizes the insecurity all new lawyers have in their ability." It is up to you to figure out where you have the depth of knowledge and confidence. Alboher has seen very young lawyers who have figured this out get senior lawyers to closely rely on them.

Like Alboher and Rootenberg, don't hide your passion. Combine it with your efforts to let others know how it contributes to your overall distinction.

SIDEBAR: Personal PR

- Look outside the law for guidance on public relations.
- Learn how to identify and customize a message that will attract the media, which can include events related to clinic activities and student organizations.
- Draft and distribute press releases to student media, hometown periodicals and alumni organizations about your accomplishments and milestones.
- Study the business of clients and prospects to enhance their PR efforts.
- Consider ways to network clients and prospects together.
- Let people know what you are doing within the law and how outside interests impact your performance.

Chapter 14
Customize

Before you ultimately decide how to promote yourself, you need to determine why you should do so in the first place. You will have to carefully select your strategy based on an in-depth self-assessment and modify it as you progress. In essence, you must learn who you are before you can decide what to become.

Some individuals thrive in a group environment and allow their personalities to naturally convey their messages. Others prefer the solitude of writing and the individualized opportunity it offers for meaningful interaction with interview subjects.

Certain law school graduates are driven by money (which is ok with me if it's ok with you), while their peers may need to contribute something to the greater good (and that means something different to everyone). Note that the two are not mutually exclusive as many well-paid large firm lawyers make extraordinary pro bono and charitable commitments. There is, however, a lifestyle decision to be made and it is one that tends to be easier to make at the outset of your career, rather than when it is in full stride.

In fact, many students who want to "make a difference" often accept positions that pay the most when the financial realities of their student loans get closer. Every professional looks back on his or her career and reflects. Those who proactively plan for their journeys tend to be more satisfied, says Paula Nailon, the Assistant Dean for Professional Development at the University of Arizona James E. Rogers College of Law and the co-author of *Excellence in the Workplace: Legal and Life Skills in a Nutshell* (Thomson, 2007). She was one of the first of a growing number of law school professional development directors in the history of legal education.

A lawyer herself, Nailon cites a report issued many years ago noting that law schools were not preparing law students for the practice of law, despite the fact that the ABA has always had language in its standards of education encouraging schools to provide students with significant opportunities to learn the practical aspects of bar membership. "Institutional change is tough and comes little by little," she says. "When I graduated from law school, I don't think I had any idea of how to lawyer," she adds.

Waiting for your school or firm to help you make personal choices is fruitless. Eventually, law schools will build business development skills into their curricula. Until they do, you need to engage in the process independently, but certainly not alone.

You have to find role models whose family values, work-life balance and success levels you can emulate. You also need to understand generational differences and where you fit on the spectrum.

The process of customizing career considerations is not that much different from buying a home. Most people start out wanting a four-bedroom center hall colonial on a tree-lined street that is conveniently located and completely renovated. Low taxes, a big backyard and a two-car garage don't hurt either. As reality sets in, a one-car garage seems sufficient and redoing the kitchen in a year or two becomes acceptable. "All of it will involve some amount of sacrifice and you have to be true to yourself," says Jackson.

STUDENTS TAKE NOTE: Start by visiting a law firm and get a sense of the environment. "Lots of people go to law school without ever having been to a law firm," says Laura Murray, a 3L at Florida International University College of Law and the Marketing Director for Miami's Bilzin Sumberg Baena Price & Axelrod. Some students try to maximize their law school experiences by working in public interest and government positions because they sense they will spend their careers in private practice. The irony in that strategy is that they will lose the opportunity to gain the experience most critical to their future success. Closet entrepreneurs may feel stifled in a law firm that restricts creative business development ideas, while men and women interested in starting families may be unhappy at firms that are less supportive of flexible scheduling.

Ask yourself the difficult questions now and incorporate the answers into some type of plan of action. Keep it simple, but address the complexity. Above all, be honest about who you are and what you would like to do (that does not just satisfy student loan providers). Be the person who is incredibly excited to get out of bed every single day (ok, at least five out of seven).

14.1 CONDUCT A SELF-EVALUATION

If you wake up looking forward to your routine, you will naturally be more successful. But, be careful because many attorneys are successful, but still yearn for something more. You can be a great lawyer in a specific field and still dislike the core subject. Developing expertise accidentally, which tends to occur when the goal is simply to find employment, could have a negative long-term impact. "Early success can be a great deodorant for dissatisfaction," advises Jackson.

While law students and junior lawyers generally have little choice about where they work, those who decide early and plant seeds that will begin to sprout upon graduation have a better chance of starting on a solid foundation. Jeff Zigler knew that he wanted to counsel health care clients, which is exactly what he is doing. Travis Hodgkins wants to counsel clients doing business in China. After a summer in Shanghai and a reputation as an insightful blogger on transnational issues, my money is on him working in that area after graduation.

Intergenerational relations in the law also play a role. New graduates are beginning to realize that marketing is a part of a lawyer's life, which is in striking contrast to their predecessors who entered the profession three decades ago. They are also adept at using electronic and web-based tools that didn't even exist until recently. "Baby Boomers and Generation Y are more team-oriented than Generation X," says Phyllis Weiss Haserot, the president of Practice Development Counsel, a business development consulting and coaching firm and the author of *The Rainmaking Machine* (West Legalworks, 2007 ed.). The current Generation Y graduates are more bold and confident in asking for help, seeking attention and touting themselves in their desire for self-expression, advises Haserot. She reports, however, they have to realize that the key to relationship building is learning about other people. She recommends asking questions more and talking about yourself less.

"Personal style trumps many other factors," adds Haserot. "Age is not necessarily the determining factor." she adds. Identify your signature style by asking your acquaintants to describe how they perceive you. Become aware of your behavioral style: your demeanor (outgoing or reserved), decision-making (quick or methodically slow), pace (fast or moderate), view of the world (big picture or detail-oriented) and focus (people-oriented or task-oriented). This will help define what is important to you and the environment in which you can optimally thrive. Learning to recognize these attributes in others will help develop relationships and enable you to address people in the ways that gain their attention.

For those of you in school or out who are not sure, start trying things on:

- Write an article in a different area of the law than that which you are currently focusing.
- Call a lawyer or business executive in the industry with whom you are unfamiliar and invite him or her to coffee.
- Read a book covering a new sector and write a review for a local magazine or newspaper (even one that is run by students).
- Attend a bar association committee meeting.

When an opportunity arises to do something different at work, seize it. If you are a corporate lawyer and a litigation partner desperately needs someone to run to court and make a simple request for an adjournment to the judge, volunteer. Fight the fear that drives complacency and take a risk. Mark Twain once said (more eloquently, of course) that people tend to regret the actions they do not take, more than those they did.

University of Houston 3L Robyn Goldstein says, "Be willing to put yourself out there." She encourages her peers to take the extra step of being proactive because it will ultimately payoff. "At a law firm, don't just do everything they tell you, take it to the next level," Goldstein advises. Those performing a self-evaluation must ask themselves how they define the next level and what that means for their personal future.

Individuals who can simultaneously balance multiple interests, or "slashers" as Alboher coined them, are generally adept at self-assessment because they are finding fulfillment from different activities. One track might offer a financial incentive, while another may nurture the body and spirit. Together they provide an appropriate level of satisfaction.

That loyalty to your life outside of the law is critical for understanding what you want and how to find it. Professionals who find themselves searching for an undefined level of satisfaction have difficulty achieving it because they often forget what drives them. "I think you bring everything you were before into your law school tenure and then you bring everything that you gained there with you into your early legal positions," says Rhonda Joy McLean, an Associate General Counsel for Time Inc. She describes law school and the practice as an intellectual discourse in which we must all engage to determine what drives us. "We are not empty vessels," she adds.

If you do not subscribe to McLean's theory, take an informal survey of your friends and contacts. Ask them whether they are doing what they want. Those that are will likely have made the determination long ago through some soul-searching process that recognized their entire background rather than a single aspect.

Realogy's Christine Baker highlights that those studying to or just entering the practice need to figure out what works best for them. "Don't force yourself into a mold that doesn't fit you," she says. McDermott's Ira Coleman takes that advice a step further and warns students not to pick an area of practice based on classes they because their impression of the work could be distorted by talented professors who make the area seem enjoyable. "You have to keep your mind open to what's not cool on TV," he advises. "There are so many areas of law that you don't know anything about and civil rights might just be one percent of your practice," he adds.

Coleman also highlights that students and lawyers alike tend to select firms for the wrong reasons. He encourages junior practitioners to look for passion and excitement in the workplace. Don't settle for less of those factors that are important to you, but again, some find those expectations unrealistic so decide for yourself.

Even forgetting the somewhat lofty elements of firm selection that Coleman suggests, Tursi Law Marketing Management's Betiayn Tursi recommends that young lawyers at least identify a firm's philosophy on business development in the early stages of one's career. "You must have a meeting with your partners and ask for expectations," she notes. "You have to find the right firm that can appreciate an associate that can develop business," she adds.

American Airlines' Clark says that while some firms want new lawyers to focus on simply honing their legal skills, it is just not enough. "You have to introduce rainmaking in your business early on," she says. It is important to understand who you are working for and what their expectations are.

The idea of rainmaking, however, is not meant to consist of handshaking and gratuitous socializing. It is much more the idea of planning now for something that may not occur for five or ten years. In the process, however, you will learn more about yourself, derive inspiration and insight from those you meet, and ultimately enjoy more of your work.

It all starts with a self-evaluation.

SIDEBAR: Self-Evaluation

- Consider your strengths, weaknesses, likes and dislikes.
- Evaluate potential jobs, fields of practice, work environments and experience based on your preferences.
- Experiment with different areas of the law and seek out opportunities to extend outside of your comfort zone.
- Control your fears and take calculated risks to more accurately assess your abilities.
- Ensure that your goals are aligned with those of your employer.

14.2 FOCUS ON CUSTOMER SERVICE

Treat people well. Period. Many of you reading that will have no idea why that comment belongs in a book about self-promotion, but it is actually critical. The manner in which you treat others is a direct reflection on your character. And, of course, character is at the heart of personal growth and professional success. "Treat everyone as you would a close friend," says Baker. This includes adversaries and support staff. "Referrals and business come from unexpected sources," she adds.

People tend to remember two types of individuals—those that say "thank you" and those that do not. Being the former is not that difficult. Even in your busiest, most stressed out or most discouraged moment, do not forget to express gratitude to those helpful to you.

Also, consider ways to manifest that gratitude. Jordan Goodman, a state and local tax attorney with Horwood Marcus & Berk in Chicago, IL, suggests that law students and even the most junior associates allow people to call them with questions, including their parents.

He teaches CLE courses on taxation and always provides his contact information. Some people will call him six times and never result in a single dollar of new business. Then one day, an attorney in Washington, D.C. called him a number of times over the course of a few months and ultimately retained him to assist on the largest case he had ever handled in his career. In the end, you just want to allow people to call you about something, he says. "You're not going to hit a home run every time, you just want to get on base," he adds. Helping them when they need help, legal or otherwise (e.g., a contact may simply need the URL to a government website containing important business forms or a way to get theater tickets while on vacation with a spouse) is generally easy and builds tremendous goodwill. Remember that referring someone to a colleague with the answer (a common point of follow-up for students and new associates) is almost as valuable as providing it yourself.

Law students who know absolutely nothing about an area of inquiry could provide an invaluable service by simply asking a professor or practitioner in his or her network about the question. And, of course, by responding quickly to the person who asked. "You have to get back to people right away," says Goodman. In an age of ubiquitous communication, that should not be too difficult. Yet it is often the smallest gestures that make the biggest impact. "If you give a time and date, and you live by it, clients are very impressed," says Goodman.

A strong believer in those impressions, he highlights that the first interaction you have with someone matters. Typos matter. Not returning a call matters. Ignoring people matters. "Those issues last a lot longer than the good stuff that you do," he cautions.

Again, there are uncomplicated ways to avoid such recognition. Review your work carefully, return calls promptly (I have never understood why this is such a problem in the legal profession, but it is pervasive), and be courteous. Eliminate bad habits before they even form. As part of your self-evaluation, you may want to identify issues with which you have trouble, such as proofreading or responding to inquiries, and work on them first. The more junior you are the greater your ability to shape the person you will become without the baggage of a reputation for carelessness or ignoring calls.

When Hanson Bridgett Partner Garner Weng was a first- or second-year associate, he defended the deposition of a mid-level executive, who was starting a company on the side. Over the lunch break, the executive asked Weng a question to which he did not have the answer. Instead of ignoring him, he contacted a colleague after their meal, but before the proceedings resumed, and provided him with the answer. The two remained in touch and when the company launched two years later, the executive retained Weng to handle his legal matters.

Weng also paid the check for lunch (and did not bill it). It was less than $15 and small gestures can leave a big impact. While he urges others to be genuinely nice to those they meet, "You cannot fake it," he says. Sometimes pretending to be polite is worse than being rude, particularly when your ruse is discovered.

Super nice doesn't have to be your thing though. "There are a lot of different ways to be successful," says Weng. "You have to find a style that suits you," he adds. The key is to incorporate a sense of customer service toward whomever it is that you are dealing with. Whether it is as simple as finding the answer to a question for a stranger or retrieving a series of cases for a partner with whom you work closely, carrying yourself with a slightly elevated level of enthusiasm can have a dramatic impact on your reputation and future.

SIDEBAR: Being Service-Oriented

- Be courteous to others.
- Find ways to manifest your gratitude.
- Make yourself available for questions and referral inquiries.
- Respond promptly.
- Pay the check.
- Demonstrate enthusiasm.

14.3 BRAND YOURSELF

While Stacey Gray was in law school and after graduation, she told everyone she met, "I am going to be the best civil rights attorney in this country." That was her sound bite. Everyone she talked to knew that she was passionate about the subject, and she demonstrated her dedication to becoming the best. She has since transitioned to high-profile and complex labor and employment matters, and her reputation for excellence remains with her many years later.

While we do not all have that kind of moxy or that level of self-assuredness, we can still brand ourselves. At Northwestern, first-years can order business cards from the Office of Student Affairs. There is a set template that students can customize with their contact information, class year and potential areas of interest. "I have heard positive comments from employers at networking events about student use of these cards," says Chamberlain. The school even offers an entire dinner to discuss etiquette, including when and how to introduce a business card into a conversation. Oklahoma City's Professor Conger also has students who have successfully used cards to make an impression on prospective employers.

"You are not going to write your phone number on a cocktail napkin," says Nancy Roberts Linder. "You are entering the profession and there is no reason you shouldn't have this critical business tool," she adds. While there are generally no rules about what goes on the card, other than anything that even remotely gives the misimpression that you are a licensed attorney if you are not, Linder recommends that students in particular use their cards as an opportunity to increase dialogue during that awkward first meeting.

Make your card different and interesting, but within the realm of professionalism. Keep your card consistent with the community in which you are engaging. If you are networking with theater producers and record executives, you may have more flexibility than if your audience is a group of commercial bankers. For instance, real estate brokers generally put their photos or other pictures on their business cards because that is an accepted practice in their industry. Lawyers do not, so you should not.

Northwestern law students have a template that ensures uniformity, but if your school does not, consider ways to make an impact. Students should seriously consider adding a personal website and blog URL to indicate their technical prowess. Those with advanced degrees should also decide whether such a reference will enhance their potential. Again, depending on your audience, an MFA may be more valuable than an MBA or PhD.

Some students targeting a particular sector could even consider creating a logo for themselves or their "brand" depending on their goals. Those seeking work in a large institutional firm should refrain from anything, but standard protocol. Others, however, who are planning to hang their own shingle or pursue a more unusual route may want to design something themselves or engage a logo design company. They are available online for as little as $200. Some companies even offer them free when you pay for business card printing (also nominally priced at under

$20). Type the term "business cards" into any search engine and you will find plenty of options.

As part of your brand, rehearse conveying your background using illustrative stories. Rather than tell others what you do, show them by visually articulating your area of interest. A patent lawyer, for example, may tell someone that she is "an inventor's best friend." This effort is similar to mastering your sound bite, but with the incorporation of something memorable. Instead of advising someone that you are the best customs lawyer, tell them a colorful tale about a client that imported a sweater featuring feathers from an endangered bird and mother of pearl buttons that caught the attention of the U.S. Fish & Wildlife Service. That will help them remember what you do (either as an intern, a summer associate or a junior lawyer). The stories are appropriate for those at any level, it is simply your impact that may be different.

If you are not a storyteller, share anecdotes about something you have in common with your audience. "If you have kids, make that your point of connection," says business development coach Arthur Levin. If you both have infants, you can lament about the sleeplessness. Share ideas about capturing key moments on film and video. There is no need to compare notes about work at all. The most successful rainmakers cultivate relationships, not clients. Clients simply end up selecting lawyers with whom they have a relationship.

Use technology to keep track of contacts and relationships, says Hubbard One's Manzo. She recommends that students and lawyers alike use a personal information manager and develop the habit of entering the names, titles, phone numbers, and unique facts about acquaintances into a database. She also recommends that everyone, students and lawyers alike, have a one-page description of what he or she does that emphasizes the benefits to the client. "It should be a short thirty-second elevator pitch that is not about you but about whom you serve," she says. "Opportunities do not always go to those who are the best in their field; they often go to those who are most organized and call you back," she adds.

The descriptions and the documents that support them are all part of your branding. They should be consistent with the message presented by your business card and any sound bite you may develop. Your reputation starts the minute you meet someone. If you want that person to remember you for something specific, make it prominent and memorable.

SIDEBAR: Branding

- Carry a business card and tailor it to the extent permitted by school, firm or ethical guidelines.
- Develop sound bites and colorful anecdotes to convey who you are and what you do clearly and concisely.
- Track your contacts in a database and record the extent of your connection.

Chapter 15
INVESTING FOR THE LONG-TERM

Despite the fact that many of us spend $100,000 or more on our legal education, it is often difficult for us to imagine that expenditure as an investment. Stacey Gray not only recognizes that fact, she suggests that law students and lawyers alike reinvest regularly. In fact, she recommends the creation of marketing budgets for memberships, trips to annual conferences, cultural activities and even a cup of coffee with someone new.

"Many law students and junior lawyers mistakenly believe that they don't have to reinvest in their professional careers," she says.

When McKesson Corporation's Jill Dessalines was a fourth-year associate in 1989 at real estate boutique Cox Castle & Nicholson in Los Angeles, John Hancock retained her to be its lawyer, the firm's only Fortune 500 client at the time. That opportunity was the direct result of attending the National Bar Association's mid-year meeting for corporate counsel. "I thought it would be a good opportunity to engage in client development," she recalls. "At the time and in the region, there were not many African-American lawyers practicing in the area of real estate," she notes. As a result, she was invited to meet with several companies looking for counsel and received her first case from John Hancock a few months later.

While her firm paid her expenses, she would have gladly done so herself given the result. She encourages law students and junior lawyers to starting thinking about creative ways to reach out into the community as soon as practicable. "There is no such thing as starting too early," she says.

Students and others who are concerned about their lack of experience and sophistication should take a cue from Dessalines' attempt. "Sometimes ignorance can actually help," she highlights. "If you don't know how daunting the task you're undertaking, you are not self-limiting," she adds.

In addition to attending legal events and continuing legal education courses, students should leverage the power of the Internet. They should have websites and promote themselves by simply updating their pages with appropriate links to their current activities.

Lenard Cohen is a Philadelphia workers compensation and personal injury attorney. He spent $500 a month on his website to promote his practice. It produced almost no results. Then in 2004, he hired Jason

Lisi, a tax attorney who founded Legal Internet Solutions Incorporated, a company that helps lawyers promote themselves online. Cohen now receives 30-50 new cases per year, the settlement of any one of which pays for his $3,000 monthly investment to optimize his website and pay-per-click advertising using Google AdWords, among other tools.

He uses pay-per-click advertising to promote his law practice, but you could use it for anything. And, while he spends thousands on his marketing, you could start with a few dollars per month. Those who develop experience in search engine techniques early in their careers will understand much more fully the nuances of organic self-promotion as they grow into the practice of law.

STUDENTS TAKE NOTE: That said, students have more freedom to experiment than associates who are operating under a law firm administration. To avoid the issue completely, consider using Google AdWords in connection with an activity that is unrelated to your work. If you are involved in a fundraiser or a political campaign, study the process in that context. In addition, while you may not have a direct opportunity to use an ad campaign of this type, your supervisor may have an interest. Check with him or her first since advertising rules in each state vary, as do interpretations for lawyer-related advertising.

The point is, of course, not to promote yourself as a law student or to plant the seeds for the great law firm brand you will someday create, but to experiment with a form of promotion that remains outside the mainstream of the legal profession. A year or more from now, something will change. You should be ready.

Investing in yourself could also be honing your technical skills for the benefit of others in the legal community. "Law students have access to technology and know what lawyers want," says prominent MyShingle blogger and Washington, D.C. solo practitioner Carolyn Elefant. She notes that law students could find ghostblogging opportunities or serve as freelance videographers for lawyers looking to experiment with on-line video. Elefant, the author of *Solo By Choice* (Decision Books, 2008), recommends that students create ways to help practicing attorneys market because they have more time and generally fewer distractions. "It is another method of building a connection," she says.

Lamenting her lack of freedom to develop a 3-4 minute YouTube-type video of her solo practice like Alison Margolin, she notes "I don't have the time to do that, but if a law student would come to me and offer a plan, I would hire him or her in a minute." In essence, Elefant urges students and junior practitioners to simply speak to people in the legal community. "See what attorneys need, package it and sell it," she says.

Again, this unusual suggestion has everything to do with learning about the needs of others in the profession and pairing your skill and enthusiasm to help them succeed. In doing so, you will find satisfaction (and perhaps some extra money), but the intent is to impact someone else's career, rather than have them impact yours. It may sound contrarian, but it is actually very consistent with the best practices of the most successful rainmakers.

Law students are more empowered today, but it is very rare for a law student to package a set of skills and be proactive, says Elefant. Doing so would certainly draw attention to you and your level of enthusiasm. Armed with a computer background, Ben Gross has been able to initiate contacts in Tucson by doing favors for others. Occasionally, he will visit the home of a friend of an acquaintance or spend a few minutes on the phone troubleshooting. "If you can do a favor for someone first, it is amazing what they will do in the future to pay you back," he says.

Take your talents, though most law students think they have few, and use them to help others do their jobs more successfully, particularly more established attorneys who are often the most difficult to reach and could be the most helpful. Gross often serves as the technical support person who helps those working from home or as they are approaching retirement.

Turns these ideas into reality by becoming a trend watcher, says Haserot. Look at new products in development and novel issues that are emerging. Study them and become an early adopter. "Older generations welcome hearing how younger people perceive the world," she says. In fact, she adds "those are ideas firms want to differentiate themselves with." Trend-watching can also present unique opportunities to work closely with a visionary senior attorney equally committed to new developments, but less connected to the twenty-something emerging community.

SIDEBAR: Investing in Yourself

- Set a marketing budget for memberships, trips to annual conferences, cultural activities and even a cup of coffee with someone new.

- Start early.
- Experiment with online tools.
- Package your skills to pracititioners who may pay you to hone them.

15.1 Prepare and Plan

While much of legal practice is learned on the job, particularly the substance, new associates that have a sense of the fundamentals of client service and satisfaction tend to be more adept at business development. That skill enables them to naturally integrate their capabilities into their early experiences. Courses like the one Bill Conger teaches at Oklahoma City University School of Law are helping to raise awareness.

Students and those just starting out need to understand their goals. It is then that they can create opportunities and measure how those opportunities fit into their plan. Nailon was specifically hired by the University of Arizona to enhance critical educational initiatives in practical skill-building for 3Ls through 8Ls (affectionately thought of as senior associates). She realized at the beginning of her tenure that reality training can start as early as the first year of school and now teaches a summer course on practice and professionalism. "It honestly prepares attendees for the workplace," she says.

As part of her effort, Nailon also connects students with the community and the state bar through mentoring and other programs. She offers CLE programming for young alumni and invites them back to the school to offer perspective to their future colleagues. "The newer generation seems more resistant to the idea of marketing," she says. "I have found that students often equate the idea of rainmaking to using people," she adds.

In addition, students are becoming increasingly shy about marketing, and often feel that it is too self-serving. Nailon cautions students against compartmentalizing their lives in the law and limiting their peer groups. Those that understand the ideas behind self-promotion and organic connections bring a unique energy and an enthusiasm to everything they do. "It is so easy to get caught up in just keeping up," Nailon says. Fight that as hard as you can.

One of her students, for example, wanted to become a prosecutor so she memorized the rules of evidence. Another wanted to develop a reputation for leadership, so he joined the local bar association's young lawyers division. "A lot of lawyers get their grounding in an organization like that," she says. "And, it eventually brings business to your firm," she adds.

SIDEBAR: Emotional Preparation for the Future

- Don't be fooled into thinking that rainmaking equates to using people or that generating organic opportunities to interact is somehow self-serving.
- Avoid any propensity for shyness and self-exclusion.
- Join the young lawyers division of a local or national bar association.

15.1.1 THE ELEMENTS OF CAREER PLANNING

Career planning is common in most institutions of higher learning. While stereotypically lost when leaving school, college graduates are often tasked with creating short- and long-term goals. These include financial, professional and personal areas. Law students, however, do not spend as much time on this process. Since a vast majority of newly minted lawyers ultimately work in a private law firm environment, large or small, their career choices are typically determined by the job they can get, rather than the job they want.

A career plan is both a manifesto for what you want to do with your life and a blueprint for building that future. It helps you decide what you want based upon your self-evaluation by setting forth specific items to help you reach a certain point. For example, after taking Nancy Roberts Linder's program at Chicago Kent in the summer of 2005, Alysia Kinsella created a personal agenda. She wrote an article about her experience for the school newspaper and joined specific associations that were set forth in her schema.

She started only attending bar association events that were interesting to her and relevant to her goals. If you attend programs aligned with your interests, you are more likely to meet with people who share your views and you will be much less inclined to cancel at the last minute (as we all tend to do with extracurricular activities of this type). In addition to relationship-building, outside events often spark creative ideas for new articles and expose one to prospects for future programs.

Kinsella suggests that students in particular create small manageable steps that they can actually accomplish. "Do not establish a plan that is too outrageous." After all, working hard at something and seeing no achievement just becomes yet another source of disappointment. Your effort may not bear immediate fruit, but accomplishment is much more powerful in the early stages than manifestation.

She had a business and creative writing background so she set a writing schedule for herself. It can be as little as one article per year. It should not be twenty-five.

We all need something to help remind us of our goals. For many rainmakers, that something is a partner with whom they can work in tandem on business development activities. For others, it can simply be an electronic calendaring system or an effort sparked by a monthly breakfast meeting.

Having a tangible career plan is not the same as writing "I will be a success" 100 times on a chalkboard. It is more like a checklist with suggested time frames. It offers one some flexible structure within which to remember the ultimate goal: to live a satisfying life and in doing so enhance your future potential to control your own destiny.

It also helps to keep you accountable to yourself and those with whom you work. If by year two on your plan (which could be your third year of law school or your second year of practice depending on when you started), you have not achieved certain milestones, you can reevaluate your decisions and modify the course. This is in direct contrast to what most people do, which is stress and worry about business development until it tends to be too late.

A career plan also helps you thoughtfully discuss your future goals with supervisors and colleagues. It not only helps you describe your plans to them, it helps you to gauge whether you are remaining true to yourself as you grow in the profession. You can also set deadlines for yourself. For example, there are certain windows of opportunity for applying to clerkships after graduation or seeking employment as a prosecutor. A plan will help you proactively prepare for these deadlines.

Sidebar: The Elements of a Career Plan

- A career plan is a manifesto for what you want to do with your life and a blueprint for building that future.
- Set manageable goals.
- Remind yourself periodically of your obligations either through a partner or using an electronic calendaring system.
- Discuss your list with supervisors and mentors.
- Use it to keep track of application deadlines and other windows of opportunity.

15.1.2 Formatting

In terms of length, it should be as long as you need it to be. If your goal is to meet one new person per month by writing two articles, hosting one panel presentation and starting an infrequent podcast, then there is not much more to note. That said, however, make every effort to include as much detail as possible in your plan. Instead of simply recording how many people you will meet, specify who those people are and include their contact information along with dates of contact. Once you record this on your plan, enter it into your electronic calendar with an e-mail reminder so that you are sure to follow up.

From a practical perspective, if you can review your career plan at a glance it is probably too short. In contrast, if you need to make time to analyze its contents, it is probably too long. Consider it an extensive list of "things to do."

You can and should modify your list as frequently as you feel it is appropriate. Do not, however, make too many changes because there should be some consistency in your program. For example, you may want to change the names of the people you are planning to meet or their order depending on certain scheduling issues, but avoid fundamentally changing the total number from twelve to one. That material change in your efforts will significantly alter the outcome and reduce valuable time.

Never make decisions based on fear of time constraints that do not yet exist. Sometimes filling your schedule with worthwhile activities gives you more time because your level of motivation is higher and your enthusiasm drives you through the day.

Look forward by looking back. As you set your goals, imagine how strongly they will impact your present and future after their completion. Ask yourself how developing relationships with the twelve new people on your list will impact your prospects after you have met them. Let that be a motivating factor and consider even noting it on your plan.

You should also update your plan as your interests and employment changes. A class in intellectual property may spark an interest in the field, which would motivate you to meet a different group of professionals or engage in one or two new activities. Similarly, a clinical project in administrative law may alter your interest in the subject.

15.1.3 PROTOCOLS

Show your plan to someone, but avoid giving it to everyone. The purpose of a career plan is to convey your goals. It is not quite revealing your hopes and dreams, but you may include ideas about starting a family, pursuing a side interest in baking cookies or taking a photography class. Share your ideas with those you trust and keep that circle of people small. The voices of too many create too much "noise" over which you cannot hear yourself think.

At least one of those individuals should be a professional contact, either a partner with whom you work closely and/or someone on your personal advisory board. Set some time on his or her schedule to review what you wrote and seek suggestions on some or all of your points of interest.

As you move forward, you can also share your victories with them. As part of your original team of confidants, he or she will have a vested interest in seeing you succeed. So, broadcast your success.

Set annual meetings to discuss changes to your plan and expectations. These meetings will help guide you as well as provide perspective to temper your level of anxiety. We are often concerned with the speed at which we achieve certain goals, when in fact we should simply be focused on the goal itself. A meeting with an advisor can encourage patience and encourage you to remain committed to the plan.

Many law firms are starting to require career planning, but these efforts can be more of an administrative exercise than a personal one. It may be that in certain circumstances you will have two plans. The first may contain specific firm-oriented goals related to billing, pro bono work, practice group support and similar functions that you discuss with an assigned individual. The second could be the one raised above, which would include career and personal goals that you address with a person of your choice.

The principal advantage of a career plan is structure, but the most significant benefit is tracking. Those individuals that have a defined set of priorities are naturally more inclined to achieve at least one of the items on their list. In fact, those who take the extra step of adding their projects to a calendar that reminds them to execute their plan are even more likely to follow-up.

A plan also serves as a tangible demonstration of your commitment to yourself and your work. It provides an example of the type of organization and thoughtfulness that you will bring to an employer or an organization. It will also keep you on track by remaining in the back of your mind as something to which you must stay loyal.

Don't review your plan as often as you obsess over your future or you will never get anything done. Evaluate your progress after each event depending on when it falls. As a rule, you should take stock of yourself every few months. Since you will be setting electronic reminders of things to do, constantly reviewing the actual career plan may be redundant.

Regardless of how often you conduct your periodic evaluation, be thorough about it. Set aside a block of uninterrupted time to consider its contents. In fact, you may want to stagger meetings with those members of your inner circle so that they fall in two or three month intervals. By doing so, you guarantee speaking with each person once per year (depending on how many you have asked for guidance) and also set forth a schedule for regular career analysis.

Periodically examining your career trajectory is no different than a regular check-up or a meeting with your financial planner. Time passes more quickly than most of us realize and every day that passes is a lost opportunity to have an impact. It is that impact that a career plan can measure and motivate. Without regular appraisal, one can easily become caught up in his or her daily routine and forget to perform the tasks most critical to shaping the future. A career plan will just remind you to stop and think every so often before you continue moving at the typical breakneck pace of modern society.

Nobody really knows how long it should take for you to get your first client or even to realize that going to law school was a good idea in the first place. Set dates and deadlines based on your instinct. You may want to build in extra time for any delays caused by finals, moot court, and, if you're lucky, some vacation. The keys are to be realistic, stay focused and maintain a healthy level of patience.

You are probably not going to achieve every goal on your list, but the purpose of including some is not the achievement, it is the attempt. Life is often much more about trying than succeeding.

Sprinkle in some easy goals with the hard one just to keep yourself motivated. For example, list lunch with a friend one month followed by coffee with the general counsel of a Fortune 500 company the next.

When you get frustrated, because we all do, seek advice. Tell people you trust that you have done X, Y and Z on your list, but are unsure how to proceed. Don't necessarily follow the suggestions that everyone provides, but draw from their experiences. Apply them to your goals.

SIDEBAR: Career Plan Protocols
- Show your plan to and discuss it with a few trusted contacts.
- Do not confuse career planning for administrative purposes with planning for personal growth.
- A well-maintained plan provides structure and a means to track progress.
- Review your plan periodically, but not too often.
- Approach frustration with patience and seek advice from someone more experienced.

15.2 TARGET YOUR AUDIENCE

In 1992, Lisa Landy was a fifth-year associate at a law firm in Miami. A high school acquaintance advised her that the Organization of Women in International Trade was establishing a Miami chapter to create a female business network. Interested, Landy called her contacts in Boston and volunteered to help form the nucleus of the organization. Three years later, the Akerman Senterfitt partner became president of the Miami chapter and in 1999 was elected chairman of the group's entire international organization. "It was very good for visibility and credibility in the local market because the media was receptive to the idea," she recalls.

Landy advises that people with common interests want to do business together. When you share character traits and expertise with others, it is easier to start a conversation and for that conversation to develop into a relationship. For that reason, she encourages law students and new lawyers to target a small number of organizations and become heavily involved with its membership.

In his second year as an associate, Andy Hahn became an active member of the Asian American Bar Association. He was interested in helping to promote more Asian American judges, rather than developing a rainmaking strategy. His enthusiasm eventually led him to chair a committee, serve on the organization's board and ultimately win an election as its president, both locally and then nationally. "There are many in-house lawyers who are involved in these bar associations," he says. "Field level in-house counsel have authority to sway business your way," he adds.

STUDENTS TAKE NOTE: While Hahn started as a second year, he recommends that students get involved while in school. It gives you a few more years of experience, develops good habits and practices, and immediately connects you with the community when you begin to practice. Many law schools have diverse bar associations and community service organizations, and if your school does not, it is a perfect opportunity to create one.

In fact, Pfizer's John Herbert encourages law students to join a cultural organization and develop creative ways of introducing their association to law firms and companies. He suggests that members invite senior lawyers and business executives to events. If you can find alumni who happen to serve in these roles, you have a distinct advantage. Herbert notes that many organizations are striving to improve their reputations for being diverse. Those who conduct business with the federal government must actually report on their relationships with diverse organizations as evidence of their efforts to diversify the workplace.

Supporting a diverse student group may be helping the corporation meet their federal requirements while simultaneously providing unique opportunities for its members to interact with high-level attorneys and executives in the private sector, he says. Similarly, Herbert notes, virtually all general counsel in the Fortune 500 have signed the ABA's pledge to ensure that diverse lawyers in firms are working on their cases. "To the extent that some of the attorneys coming out of law school can help to promote that type of diversity, they become assets to the law firm in terms of developing new client bases."

Despite the tendency to join many groups, Landy cautions students against that strategy. She had initially joined many organizations and was overwhelmed with monthly meetings that served almost no purpose in her career plan. "You get business from your friends and those people who have faith in your abilities," she says. "It is, therefore, much better to be involved in a few key organizations."

That principle applies to most activities, not simply organizational involvement. If you are a blogger, focus on subjects in which your audience has an interest. The same is true if you are podcasting, attending conferences or arranging panels. Associate yourself with a topic and even a theme. Gabe Galanda is the person to speak with about Indian law, while Ira Coleman is an authority on legal issues in healthcare transactions. They designed it that way. You can do the same.

When you first begin the process, however, it is perfectly acceptable to experiment with subjects, personalities and fora. "You have to find what you're good at, find your niche and strengthen yourself in that area," says Robyn Goldstein. When you try different items on and determine whether they fit, you can whittle down your efforts to those that will bear the most fruit and lead to the greatest satisfaction.

"Find something that lights you up more than anything else," says Coleman. He was intrigued by whether physicians should own side businesses to which they refer patients. He enjoyed the ingenuity inherent in advising on creative strategies. "Discover a topic that motivates you intellectually or socially on which you could spend time and gain some expertise," he adds. When you're passionate, you will be better. And, when you're better, you're more likely to make an impact.

Coleman also recommends that when starting out, consider moving off the beaten path to distinguish yourself. When legislators and lawyers were studying the legal implications of new restrictions from the perspective of managed care plans, Coleman studied the physician's angle. "It was not as big an audience or client base, but it was easier to get clients," he says. The managing partner of McDermott's Miami office lectured to students graduating from their resident programs. Some of those students became clients who ultimately went on to be Chief Executive Officers of public companies.

ASSOCIATES TAKE NOTE: Weil, Gotshal's Adam Hemlock learned this early as an associate. Rather than being unrealistic in terms of business development expectations at a top-tier law firm, he focused on clients with whom he had regular contact. He cultivated relationships with the junior employees and left the senior members of the client teams to connect with the partners. "Focus on the junior and mid-level people who will eventually be selecting counsel," he suggests.

Hemlock was seconded for two years from Weil in New York to Yokohama, Japan as senior legal counsel for Panasonic Mobile Communications and continues to work extensively with Panasonic and other Japanese clients. He kept in touch with people in Japan and considers many of those with whom he worked true friends. "I always make sure to work hard and give good service," he says. Simply building relationships is more realistic for junior associates than swinging for a home run, he adds.

When those relationships are founded on common interests, their potential for longevity is much greater.

SIDEBAR: Directing Your Efforts

- Promote your involvement in a culturally diverse organization to enhance the potential for guest speakers and local law firm sponsorship.
- Focus on a small number of manageable activities and organizations to maximize your impact.
- Interact with others at your level of experience.
- Before choosing groups or topics on which to focus, divide your time between a diverse array.
- Find your passion and pursue it enthusiastically.
- Look off the beaten path for ways to distinguish yourself.

15.3 Build a Rainmaking Team

When Cathy Fleming attends a meeting with a prospective client, a networking function or even a bar association dinner, she does so with a partner. "Never ever market alone," she urges. While she recommends that attorneys at least market in pairs, they could even work in larger numbers. The idea behind the team approach is that your colleagues will not let you off the hook for engaging in activities that exceed your comfort level. They will encourage and even pressure you to overcome your discomfort. Fleming suggests that students and junior associates bring friends or co-workers with them to every event. Set goals before you attend and at its conclusion hold each other accountable.

That accountability should be positive, but honest and constructive. If one or both of you did not achieve certain goals, study the reasons for your deficiency and suggest ways to improve on your next attempt. "People make mistakes, so make them," says David Leffler. He notes that even the smoothest among us start out doing it terribly. "Just accept it because that is how you learn, and don't let that stop you," he adds.

It is much easier to enter a room with a friend than alone. You may be inclined to remain with that friend out of nervousness, but your pre-set goals should break you away from that crutch. Take chances while they mean almost nothing and they still offer you virtually total upside. You have no pressure to build a book of business or impress anyone with your rainmaking prowess. All you have to do is be yourself and enjoy the experience. Afterward, make a few notes and attempt to improve the next time.

Associates Take Note: Fleming also highlights, "It is much easier to sell your partner than to sell yourself." So as part of your strategy, consider opportunities to compliment your partner and underscore his or her capabilities and/or accomplishments. This requires that you both (or all, depending on the size of your contingent) learn about one another so that you can capably convey that to a prospective audience.

"Teamwork is key," says Hemlock, who strongly believes in a group dynamic for developing business and cultivating relationships. "Clients at major firms are far too sophisticated to have one individual be everything," he advises. He works with a few other partners in various disciplines who develop business in Japan. As a team, they are far more successful than if each acted alone. As Fleming suggests, he is quick to promote the skill and experience of his partners because his goal is to bring work to the firm as a whole, rather than to himself.

From an in-house perspective, Andrea Clark suggests that new associates introduce prospects to more seasoned lawyers at their firms. "Adding other people to your team who can assist you is key to landing a client," she notes.

More practically, however, Fleming says, "It is much easier to forgive yourself than to have others forgive you, if you don't do what you say." For that reason, she encourages tandem effort and evaluation.

SIDEBAR: Rainmaking in Teams

- Try to connect with others in pairs or groups.
- You have no pressure to produce results so enjoy the process and identify your strengths and weaknesses.
- Promote the skills and talents of others.

Chapter 16
THINK OF OTHERS

When Kirk Rose was being considered for his current position as the Chief Financial Officer for Global Hyatt Corporation in Chicago, the selection committee received an unsolicited recommendation in support of his candidacy. It was from an attorney who hired Rose out of law school many years before. The plug certainly did not hurt his chances. "Law students need to be mindful of the impressions that they make," he says.

One of the hallmarks of success and a common signature among rainmakers is not only that they are genuinely considerate human beings, but also that they proactively think of others. And, those others tend to remember their efforts.

This could be as simple as wishing someone a happy birthday, yet it could include referring new business, helping promote someone's venture or donating money to a charitable event he or she is sponsoring. Of course, this is all done with absolutely no expectation of any return whatsoever. Consider it an indirect investment in your future. The energy and time commitment for these activities is typically minimal and the potential return can impact your career.

Baker Botts partner Dennis Duffy retained his first client as a 28-year-old junior associate. He had been in communication with the in-house lawyer at a large corporation for six months. "I decided that I had to be able to give something of value," he recalls. That value was simply reading slip-opinions relating to the corporation's industry. If he saw anything relevant, he sent it along. "It was basically saying, 'I am thinking about you,'" Duffy adds. The in-house counsel ultimately decided that Duffy understood enough of what was important to him to represent him. "My communications with that client made a big difference," he says.

16.1 REWARD WITH AWARDS

Thoughtfulness is often simply recognition of the good work of others. It is a genuine effort to acknowledge that certain people are motivating and even inspiring in their efforts, which are worthy of peer celebration. It can be simple and quiet, but it is often very meaningful.

Propelled by the success of their self-published magazine, Raskin Peter, PWC and Korn Ferry created The Counselor, an award to recognize the entertainment industry's in-house counsel at an annual Media and Entertainment Counsel of the Year Awards dinner. The three companies convinced global law firm, Foley & Lardner LLP, to agree to be the ceremony's first sponsor in the fall of 2005 and held an awards dinner. Although they presented only three awards, they received nominations from around the world, including Germany, India and Mexico, with a total of over one hundred candidates. The winners were: the General Counsel of Sony Pictures Entertainment; the Commissioner of the Arena Football League; and, the General Counsel of the United States Anti-Doping Agency.

In 2007, the awards show recognized figures in twelve categories, such as Rising Star, Deal Maker and Video and On-Line Games Counsel, among others. It was held at the Friars Club in Beverly Hills and sold out its two hundred tickets more than six months in advance. The Hollywood Reporter was the media partner and the General Counsel of Intel was the program's keynote speaker.

"It has opened a lot of doors," says Peter, who represents a variety of entertainment industry clients in litigation and transactional matters. The association, the magazine and the awards show have given him and his founding colleagues direct access to the decision makers in his field, prominence and the ability to co-brand each other and, of course, new clients. "People want to work with those they know, which is especially critical in the entertainment industry," he adds. More people are sure to know him since The College of Law Practice Management recognized Peter's firm with a 2007 InnovAction Award for excellence and innovation in the management and delivery of legal services.

Arnold Peter and his team turned a straightforward idea into a coveted and lavish event. While that is possible for you, it may not be necessary for your purposes. Law students and junior associates can simply recognize those they respect by creating an annual or semi-annual award from their particular organization. People like awards, particularly for worthy efforts that are often ignored.

To make the impact effective, surround it with a credible process where you evaluate various candidates made up of people that you would like to meet. Decide on one (or more if that is appropriate) based on preset criteria. Then, let the recipient know that you would like to grant the award in his or her name.

Those acting on their own can cite someone in his or her blog, spotlight them on a podcast or profile that person in an article series about award-worthy individuals. Your goal should be to find ways to spotlight individuals who do great work.

Magazines often devote entire issues to "Lawyers of the Year" or "40 Under 40." You can do the same in whatever your capacity. In fact, entire law firms can evaluate clients and in-house counsel to select one or more for some type of accolade. Consider suggesting that to your firm management or the law firm marketing professionals with whom you have become acquainted.

The people you select do not have to be lawyers. Consider diversifying your nominees to expand your exposure and to enhance the creative nature of the project. Reward artists and musicians if you like, as well as faculty and fellow students. Since many of your classmates and colleagues will ultimately be the in-house counsel with whom you will want to connect in six or eight years, leave a lasting impression by granting them appreciation for a meaningful effort in which they may be engaged. After all, everyone loves to list accolades on their resumes.

SIDEBAR: Awards
- Awards help acknowledge the motivating and inspiring efforts of others.
- The award can be small and given to multiple individuals.
- Use uniform criteria to make your selection.
- Spotlight both lawyers and non-lawyers.

16.2 BE ACTIVE LOCALLY

Law school tends to be a transient environment with students shuttling back and forth between their original hometowns and campus. Some are close by and others could be thousands of miles away. That said, however "the world is fairly small," notes Rose, which is why he encourages students and new members of the bar to become active in their communities.

For students attending school locally, get involved with issues that have personal meaning to you. It could be staying connected to a rural sports team or helping to fight homelessness in New York City. The key is often your way of remaining connected, rather than the central theme motivating you to do so. Leaving home for three years can put you at a distinct disadvantage when you return.

Consider becoming a correspondent of some type for a local or regional publication. A blog may even serve the same purpose in this effort. Stay linked to local government issues by checking municipal websites and volunteering for events when you are in the area. In modern society, proximity is less significant so suggest ways to be useful without being personally available. Plant seeds when you leave so that they will sprout upon your return. "Starting when you are twenty-five gives you a huge advantage over other people," says Rose.

Bill Conger instructs his students to build a profile in their communities so that they develop a three-dimensional image. "People will see you as civic-minded and doing your duty," he notes. "Then they will judge you as a lawyer as well."

16.2.1 RUN FOR PUBLIC OFFICE

Twenty-nine-year-old Rodney Glassman planned to practice after graduation in December of 2007, but lined up another job on November 6, 2007 when he won the Ward 2 seat on the Tucson City Council for which he ran during his last semester in law school. He raised the $45,000 maximum permitted by law for his race through 2,250 contributions of $20 each (even I sent him twenty bucks just because I appreciated his chutzpah). He is purportedly the first candidate in history to do so. "You don't just want to give everyone a seat at the table," he says. "You want an equal seat at that table."

Glassman provides a great example of what is possible with some creativity. Even before graduation, he was one of the most prominent individuals in Tucson and perhaps the state of Arizona because of his campaign.

He focused his efforts with laser precision on his local community, letting its members know what he supports. (His website notes that he is "passionate about protecting our Sonoran desert, advocating on behalf of working families, creating new opportunities for children, assisting seniors in maintaining their independence, and ensuring a high quality of life.") He also hosted his own public access cable television show called "Consider This," on which he addressed community issues and featured guests such as the Tucson Chief of Police.

While I have already noted the benefits of producing your own cable show, consider Glassman's opportunities to leverage his reputation and broaden his name recognition by running for office. First, he convinced 2,250 people (some of whom he knew personally, many of whom he did not) to mail checks for $20 to his campaign. Second, he was the co-host with local leaders of numerous events to mark milestones in his effort. For example, a local county sheriff helped host his primary election kick-off party. Third, he had a platform on which to communicate with the entire community. He encouraged everyone to vote, whatever their choice, demonstrating an honest interest in empowerment, rather than simply a desire to win. Fourth, he sponsored socially responsible interaction by giving volunteers opportunities to operate phone banks and canvas neighborhoods on his behalf. Best of all, they helped to distribute "small tasteful yard signs" for display throughout the city. Naturally, all of them featured the candidate's name in large type.

Brooklyn Law School professor David Reiss ran for a New York City Council seat in the 33rd District covering parts of Brooklyn in 2001 when he was a mid-level associate at Paul, Weiss, Rifkind, Wharton & Garrison demonstrating that the effort is possible even when one does not have the luxury of a law student's schedule.

Reiss does, however, caution that running for public office may be inconsistent with a future in a large national law firm. "The benefits of running to your legal career depend on what you want," he says. While it takes you out of the anonymous group from the class of 2007 and gives you individuality, the demands of the big firm life cannot be balanced with running for office in a serious way, he adds. It effectively gives future employers a six-month interview of you to see how you behave under pressure, and to see your strengths and weaknesses. As such, you have to remember to present yourself in a way that you want to be seen in professional life.

Reiss highlights that rainmakers and politicians are doing the same thing. "They have a constituency and are trying to help that constituency solve a problem," he notes. In fact, Pfizer's Herbert suggests that "law students are probably better off nurturing partisan relationships" because they can cultivate that interaction throughout their entire careers.

Regardless of your position on that point, there are few more powerful ways to establish yourself in local politics than running for office when an opportunity arises.

Just as Reiss was finishing his campaign, another associate arrived at Paul Weiss with similar notions of public service. Fresh off of a federal clerkship, Daniel Garodnick, who grew up on Manhattan's east side, began preparing to run for a seat on the New York City Council in 2003 (at thirty-one years old). He was elected in the fall of 2005 and notes that running for office as an associate required a delicate balance. "The connections that people can make and opportunities that the law firm can present help you to establish the network necessary to become better known," says Councilman Garodnick.

Those connections can be both professional and personal. In the course of his community involvement, Garodnick became friends with New York State Assemblyman Jonathan Bing. When Bing married Meredith Ballew, the executive director of Wall Street Rising, in September of 2005, Garodnick was his best man. In fact, "I met my wife through politics and would not have met her had I not run for office," says Bing.

Before his election in November of 2002, Bing was an associate with Torys LLP and was the New York Coordinator of the Federal Emergency Management Agency/American Bar Association's Disaster Legal Services following the attacks of September 11, 2001. "It is important for lawyers to be involved in their community and to give something back to those who helped you get to where you are," he says.

The Assemblyman notes that whether one is a student, associate or solo practitioner, it is important to have a well-rounded life. "Starting out in practice is like being a freshman in college," he says. "You sign up for everything and figure out which activities can be most beneficial to you." Almost all bar associations have young lawyers groups, which is how he became involved in guiding the direction of the profession. He started on the governing body for the New York State Bar Association and then joined the American Bar Association's House of Delegates. He also encourages pro bono activities noting that his work after 9/11 proved to him that government could make a positive difference in the lives of its people.

Glassman himself gained prominence as a future political figure with a high moral character (he is an Eagle Scout) and made headlines for his fairness in fundraising. More importantly, he is now a known and recognized figure. He mastered the art of genuine organic self-promotion. And, he has done it with honesty and integrity by promoting the issues that are important to others while volunteering to be their spokesman. When asked during his campaign about higher office, Glassman noted, "One can run for mayor anytime, but I have to finish law school now."

The Glassman model can be easily adapted to law school or a local bar association, so do not be intimidated by the idea of running for a city council seat. Campaigning out of interest to serve any community, regardless of its size or demographic, can offer the very same benefits. Student bar association and practitioner bar association presidents enjoy many of the same benefits as public office holders.

"Politics is politics in a small P sense," says A. Michael Pratt, a partner with Pepper Hamilton LLP and Chancellor of the 13,000-member Philadelphia Bar Association. Pratt notes that once an individual interested in running for anything is internally standing out as a person with skills and a strong work ethic, he or she must meet people to persuade them of the value of his or her candidacy. "Identify who the big players are, sometimes the small players, that you need to reach out to," he suggests. Also consider organizations from which you need support. In Philadelphia, for example, a Chancellor-hopeful needs backing from a diverse group of bar associations, the trial lawyers association, and the young lawyers division. For those just starting out, Pratt notes, "Even if you have asked them to support you and they support someone else, you may be able to impress them as someone with leadership ability for a future run."

At the end of the day, you are going to meet a lot of people who will remember your name. "For young people who enter politics, it is a no-lose proposition," says New York State Assemblyman Hakeem Jeffries, who was an associate at Paul Weiss with Councilman Garodnick. "As long as you run a campaign that is decent and ethical, it allows you to present some of the favorable traits that you possess," adds Jeffries, who launched his first campaign at thirty when he was a third-year associate.

Like Garodnick, Jeffries campaigned at subway stations for two hours from 7:00 to 9:00 every morning. He worked in the firm's midtown Manhattan office from 9:30-5:30 and then returned to his district between 6:00 and 6:30 to attend community meetings and knock on doors. On most nights, he would return to the law firm to finish his work, often burning the midnight oil. He only took a leave of absence during the final three months of his campaign.

Start by just showing up at some events, says Pratt. Get onto an outside project with a very narrow purpose that takes little of your time. People will support you when you have paid your dues.

Finally, you need to have the support of your employer, remarks Pratt. "Without that, it is very difficult to succeed at both."

SIDEBAR: Getting Involved

- Build a profile in your community to develop a three-dimensional image.
- Running for public office has certain challenges that may be inconsistent with employment in a large law firm.
- Candidates can convey their message to an entire consituency at once.
- Consider nurturing political relationships.
- Rainmakers and politicians use similar skills.
- Many of the benefits of running for office are available to those seeking positions within the ABA or even a student bar association.

16.2.2 SERVE ON BOARDS AND COMMISSIONS

For those not inclined to embark on a political campaign, DirecTV's Warren Jackson also recommends serving on local boards and commissions. Their focus can range from the arts and culture to human rights and the environment. Jackson served on the Los Angeles Police Commission and the city's Civil Service Commission. "It is a great way to raise your profile within the municipality where you are," he says.

STUDENTS TAKE NOTE: Doing so generally requires an application of interest and some experience in the subject. Law students may be interested in serving on the civilian complaint review board or a generic public service committee. Those new to local politics may want to seize any opportunity regardless of the subject area. Even an undesirable position on an obscure commission, for example, could give you the chance to offer leadership and volunteer to handle the more burdensome and time-consuming tasks for which the other members do not have the time.

Sometimes law schools themselves will offer opportunities to serve on steering committees or provide for non-voting student membership to faculty appointment groups. Look for ways to get involved that do not require significant time commitments, but provide exposure to group work performed by consensus.

Local chapters of national bar associations, local bars, and non-profits are also great sources of these prospects. Ask your mentor and others within your circle how to learn more and get involved.

STUDENTS TAKE NOTE: Christine Brady is a 4L in the William S. Boyd School of Law at the University of Nevada, Las Vegas. She was the school's ABA representative and is now the liaison to the ABA Section of Legal Education and Admissions to the Bar. "By meeting all of these people, it opens up the world," she notes. Houston 3L Robyn Goldstein is on the board of governors serving as an ABA Circuit Governor for the 13th circuit representing Texas and Louisiana. "It has afforded me many opportunities," she says.

The American Bar Association offers students an excellent start in terms of leadership, but with a creative focus and a broad view, those studying and practicing can find many occasions to serve.

SIDEBAR: Boards & Commissions
- Serving your community helps to raise your profile.
- Local bar association chapters and non-profit organizations offer great opportunities to gain experience.
- Seek advice from your mentor on how to get more involved.

16.3 BE CHARITABLE

Before he became a city council member, Rodney Glassman was known for being the founder of an eponymous charity. With a $2,000 loan from an ice-skating rink at which he was a general manager, he started the Glassman Foundation in 2002. His goal was to raise money for organizations devoted to helping children in southern Arizona. He also wanted to promote positive community involvement among teenagers in the region. It now donates over $150,000 annually to various area non-profits by fundraising at events that include musical entertainment (Glassman is himself is a respected soprano), a community roast, and a youth poker tournament, among various other activities.

According to Glassman, his charitable work has given him the ability to link law school students with prominent alumni who have appeared at his charity events. In addition, "being engaged in the community is great because it puts me on the radar for firms," he says. Glassman actually established his first roast to get to know local businesspeople and encourage them to help selected charities.

He encourages other students and practitioners to start with a small effort. "Fundraisers are contagious," he says. "Once you attend one, you want to have your own," he adds. To make an impact, you do not need to create an entire organization through which to distribute hundreds of thousands of dollars. You can start a children's book drive or collect one-dollar donations to purchase gifts for children at a nearby hospital. Like Glassman, you will build on each effort and expand as you generate interest.

The act of trying is the critical factor in an endeavor of this nature. It gives you a genuine excuse to contact local attorneys and businesspeople. Connect with those who support similar interests. Building bonds through socially responsible ventures generates meaningful interaction based on common character traits. Those traits dictate who works with whom and often who retains whom to be their lawyer. It also gives you the chance to get to know someone outside the legal community and as a person that is committed to society in the same way that you are.

It can also help you highlight your firm's work and its values, says Ross Fishman. He cites examples of a personal injury firm that handles motor vehicle accidents, which helps fund drunk driving prevention programs, and an international law firm serving as the primary sponsor of the Russian Ballet's local appearance. "Make a real difference of which everyone can be proud." Like Glassman, he suggests putting a human face on the contribution.

SIDEBAR: Charity
- Start small and encourage participation by attorneys and businesspeople within the community.
- Encourage participation by classmates and colleagues.
- Remember, the effort is much more important than any success.

Chapter 17
The Choice

This book is chock full of ideas, but don't be overwhelmed. (I can't believe you made it through either.) It is, however, time to make a decision. Are you willing to take some risk for the potential of much greater reward? Rather than asking yourself whether you have the time to take action, ask yourself whether you have the time not to.

The book does not suggest that you change everything you are doing. Rather, it offers ideas for incorporating a new routine that recognizes the importance of organic relationship-building and regular self-evaluation. It is meant to encourage your pursuits while thinking of others as much as, if not more than, yourself.

You have the opportunity to take a giant leap toward becoming whatever it is that you want. It should start in law school, but it never ends there. Explore, learn and experiment. Meet, discuss and share. There are certain qualities that those who have achieved, and continue to achieve success, share: They are interested in others; they relentlessly pursue knowledge and experience; and, they are willing to take risks (at least the calculated kind).

And after all, "There are very few risks that will result in catastrophic results," says Dale & Thomas Popcorn co-founder Richard Demb. If you start with that premise, there is little to lose and much to gain. Getting started is so difficult because most law students and junior lawyers believe that they are not yet at the point when they need to start thinking about organic self-promotion. Those that do not, however, are at a significant disadvantage.

Start with something small. Ask a friend or another trusted contact to introduce you to the two most interesting people he or she knows. In this book, I have introduced you to 100.

The irony about the type of initiative suggested here is that it is productive and fun. Everything mentioned is effective and some may even say, "inspiring." If it doesn't work, you've learned your first lesson about success: It always comes with a little bit of failure thrown in for good measure. The funny thing about failure is that it ends up being a great story later on.

How cool would it be to host a panel of the most impressive lawyers, business professionals, musicians or whomever? What about interviewing twenty-something entrepreneurs or newly elected public officials on your own public access cable television show? How about a simple cup of coffee with a writer who likes to have coffee with people? (Ok, maybe that last one was a stretch, but you get my point.)

As many in this book have recommended, focus on what and whom you like. Become interesting and enthusiastic because it is infectious. "Always have a story," says Demb. "People like to hear stories; they don't appreciate lost souls."

If nothing else, the ideas outlined in these chapters give some direction on maximizing your experience in the law, whether you are still studying it or finally practicing. Attorneys that wait until they become partner or senior associates lose some of the opportunity to enjoy the sense of adventure. In fact, if given the chance, many would return to law school or their first few years of practice and take some of the steps I have outlined.

If you try something and it doesn't work out, what do you lose? Organic self-promotion is unique in that if done properly, there is no defeat. If your goal is to meaningfully connect with others, demonstrate who you are by learning about who they are, and discover unanticipated opportunities, you always win.

So take a shot.

While you're at it, throw a hundred bucks monthly into a mutual fund and call me on your 65th birthday.

I will send you an umbrella.